Complete
Meditation

222 questions

Complete
Meditation
From doing meditation to being meditation

SIRSHREE
Author of the bestseller *The Source*

Complete Meditation
By **Sirshree** Tejparkhi

Copyright © Tejgyan Global Foundation
All Rights Reserved 2007

Tejgyan Global Foundation is a charitable organization
with its headquarters in Pune, India.
ISBN : 978-81-906627-6-5

Published by WOW Publishings Pvt. Ltd., India

Fifth edition published in November 2011

Third reprint published in February 2025

Printed and bound by Trinity Academy For Corporate Training Ltd, Pune

Copyright and publishing rights are vested exclusively with WOW Publishings Pvt. Ltd. This book is sold subject to the condition that it shall not by way of trade or otherwise, be lent, resold, hired out, or otherwise circulated without the publisher's prior written consent in any form of binding or cover other than that in which it is published and without a similar condition including this condition being imposed on the subsequent purchaser and without limiting the rights under copyright reserved above, no part of this publication may be reproduced, stored in or introduced into a retrieval system, or transmitted, in any form, or by any means, electronic, mechanical, photocopying, recording or otherwise, without the prior written permission of both the copyright owner and the above-mentioned publisher of this book. Any person who does any unauthorized act in relation to this publication may be liable to criminal prosecution and civil claims for damages.

Although the author and publisher have made every effort to ensure accuracy of content in this book, they hereby disclaim any liability to any party for any loss, damage, or disruption caused by errors or omissions, resulting from negligence, accident, or any other cause. Readers are advised to take full responsibility to exercise discretion in understanding and applying the content of this book.

Contents

Preface	Those who have eyes should read, those who have ears should listen...! 222 Questions	9
PART I	**MEDITATION FOR BEGINNERS**	**13**
Chapter 1	What Is Meditation, What Is Not Meditation Five Important Questions	15
Chapter 2	Necessities of Meditation Posture, Time, Place, Mudra	21
Chapter 3	What is Meditation Meditation and Mind	29
Chapter 4	Twelve Benefits of Meditation Physical, Mental, Spiritual	35
Chapter 5	Three Stages of Meditation Pure Mind, Quiet Mind, No Mind	41
Chapter 6	Six Steps of Meditation The Power of the Subdued, Focused and Aware Mind	47
Chapter 7	How to Meditate Thoughts, Sleep, Dreams	63
Chapter 8	Questions on Meditation Misconceptions about Meditation	73
PART II	**MEDITATION FOR SEEKERS**	**85**
Chapter 9	From Meditation to Self Meditation The Real Goal	87
Chapter 10	Witness – Self-Witness Language And Words	111

PART III	**MEDITATION FOR DISCIPLES**	**115**
Chapter 11	**First Truth**	
	Sense of Being	117
Chapter 12	**The Importance of Understanding in Meditation – Part I**	
	Understanding and Listening	133
Chapter 13	**The Importance of Understanding in Meditation – Part II**	
	God and I	147
PART IV	**MEDITATION FOR MEDITATORS**	**151**
Chapter 14	**Self Meditation and Wasted Meditation**	
	Techniques and Obstructions	153
PART V	**MEDITATION FOR DEVOTEES**	**167**
Chapter 15	**Samadhi**	
	Understanding and Conviction	169
Chapter 16	**Who Am I**	
	'Who Am I' Meditation	181
Chapter 17	**The Method and Techniques of Meditation**	
	Seven Meditation Techniques	189
	Glossary	**204**
	Appendices	**209**

• HOW TO DERIVE MAXIMUM BENEFIT FROM THIS BOOK •

1. Read the book in a sequential order. (Read the first part first, the second part second, and so on).
2. Avoid comparing the answers given in this book with the information that you have already accumulated in the past.
3. Derive maximum benefit from this book by understanding your current stage (i.e. whether you are a beginner, seeker, disciple, meditator, or devotee) and your aim.
4. The profound thoughts or quotes that are given at the beginning and end of each chapter are meant for contemplation. Contemplate deeply on them.
5. First decide your goal – whether you want to attain benefits, understanding, meditation, Self Meditation or *Samadhi* – and then begin reading this book.
6. If questions arise in your mind while reading this book, then write them down immediately. These questions will be subsequently answered as you continue reading the book.
7. Note down your experiences in a diary and keep a record of your progress in meditation in a chronological order. Do not meditate in front of others to show off. Meditation is meant for annihilating the ego, not for perpetuating the disease of ego.

Note :
This book is a compilation of answers given by Sirshree in response to questions asked by various seekers at various times.

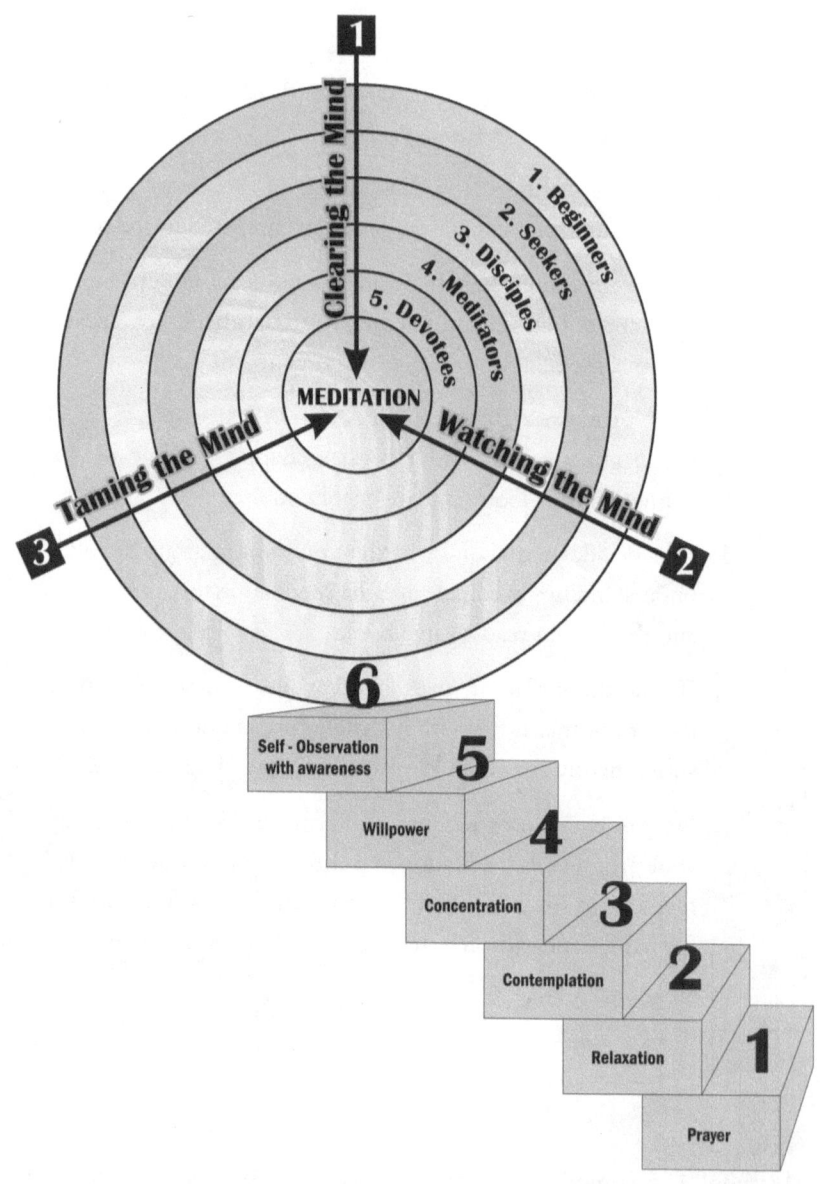

PREFACE

Those who have eyes should read, those who have ears should listen...!
222 QUESTIONS

If we believe that whatever is inside our skin is "I"
and everything outside our skin is not "I",
then meditation breaks this belief of ours.

Can you invest half your life to know how to live the remaining half of your life?

Can you invest half your wealth to learn how to spend the remaining half?

If the answer to both these questions is 'yes', then this book is for you. You can derive maximum from it.

If the answer to both these questions is 'no', then this book is a 'must read' for you.

'Those who have eyes should read' implies that those who have the eye of discernment (*parakh*), the ability to discriminate between the truth and untruth, should read. 'Those who have ears should listen' implies that those who have intense thirst for the truth and are prepared to listen intently should listen. Many a time we see what we want to see and we hear what we want to hear. For example, there is a signboard in a garden that reads: *Plucking flowers is prohibited*. Somebody uproots the whole plant and declares, "I have not violated the instruction. I have not plucked the flowers." Such a person, even after reading, is actually not reading.

Some people have the habit of jumping to conclusions after listening to just a word or a sentence. For this reason, they are never really ready to listen, understand or think anything new. Whenever something new is said, they reject it. Consequently they stop listening to the truth and lose out on all further possibilities. Therefore, make a resolution before reading this book that you will not jump to conclusions or make any presumptions. This means that you will read and understand the content as it is, without comparing it with your previous knowledge.

In this book, Tejguru Sirshree has answered questions regarding meditation in the journey from 'beginner to devotee'. It consists of five main parts, three stages and six steps of meditation, which have been presented in the form of 222 questions. The purpose is to solve the questions of most people and to answer questions of seekers at every stage. Besides this, the book includes the following: Definition of meditation, Wealth of meditation, Prerequisites for meditation, Twelve benefits of meditation, Stages of meditation, Steps of meditation, How to meditate, Questions-Answers related to meditation, From Meditation towards Self Meditation, Witness – Self-Witness, Importance of 'understanding' in meditation, Self Meditation and wasted-meditation, Samadhi, Seven meditation techniques, as well as a survey on meditation.

To make a subject such as meditation simple and clear, it has been divided into five parts. The first part is mainly for those who are not familiar with meditation. The other four parts are for those who are already accustomed to meditation techniques. The answers, which have been given for beginners in the first part have changed in the subsequent four parts. Therefore, new seekers are requested not to draw conclusions after reading just the first part by thinking, 'This is for us… or this is not for us.' Some parts of the text have been repeated with the purpose of explaining the subject in depth; please do not neglect this. The speciality of Tej Gyan Foundation is that whatever knowledge is imparted here is presented in a very simple, easy, and unique manner.

Every belief is broken here, be it ever so beautiful, because even if handcuffs are made of gold, they still are the cause of bondage. Likewise, even though a belief appears very beautiful, yet it is the cause of ignorance.

Editor's Note : In the text, some words have been added in brackets in order to bring out the meaning relevant to the given context. It has been attempted to accurately represent the content which was originally delivered in the Hindi language. For this reason, at some places there is repetition of sentences as is common in spoken language and at some places the language used in this book may deviate from the standard grammatical norms. A humble request of forgiveness is made to the reader for any such lapses.

MEDITATION
REFERENCE LIST OF QUESTIONS

Titles	Question No.	Titles	Question No.
1)	Posture – (Q.6) 1	18)	Thoughtless – 39-48
2)	Concentration – 69-72, 88, 103, 104	19)	Disadvantages – 91-94
		20)	Prayer – 31
3)	Self Realisation – 97	21)	Light – 199, 200
4)	Meditation – 1, 2, 9, 78	22)	Time (Q.6) 3
5)	God – 173-184	23)	Breath – 7, 57, 67, 188
6)	Guru – 105, 118	24)	Place – (Q.6) 4
7)	Mistakes – 111	25)	Willpower – 35
8)	Emptiness – 49, 50	26)	Samadhi – 96, 205-212
9)	Aim – 115, 116	27)	Self Meditation – 79, 80, 187, 192, 197
10)	Benefits – 20-27, 204		
11)	Mudra – (Q.6) 2	28)	Relaxation – 32
12)	Contemplation – 33, 73, 167	29)	Understanding – 102, 168, 169-172, 214
13)	Mind (Subconscious mind) 11-19, 28, 29, 30, 34, 36, 68, 108, 129, to 134, 141, 146, 153, 194, 198		
		30)	Self – 145, 147, 149, 151
		31)	Witness – 113, 117
		32)	Contrast mind – 197, 198
14)	Moun – 158	33)	Wasted meditation – 3, 4, 190, 191
15)	False Beliefs – 54		
16)	Body-Mind Mechanism – 134, 136, 139, 189	34)	Meditation techniques – 5, 81, 201, 202 and chapter 17
17)	Who Am I? – 119, 143, 185, 186, 218-222	35)	Present – 56

Complete Meditation • 12

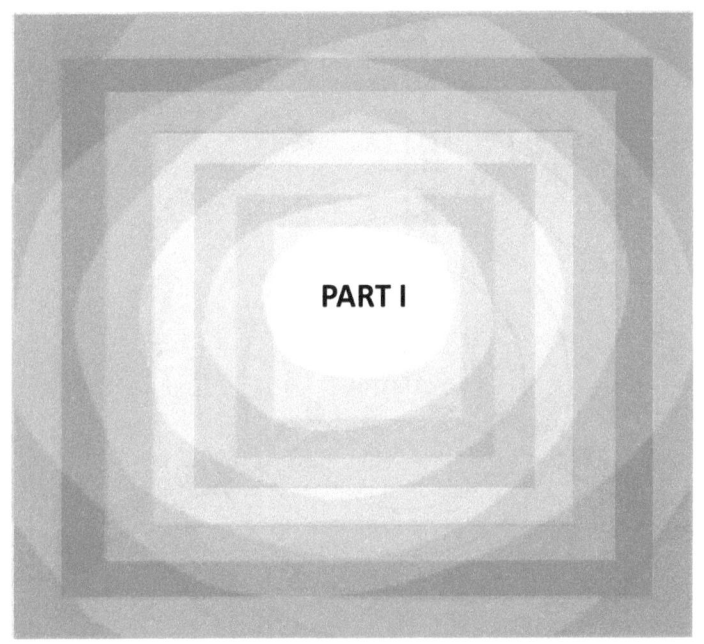

PART I

MEDITATION FOR BEGINNERS

A beginner is one
who has just become ready to learn.
His questions are essential
for beginning with meditation.

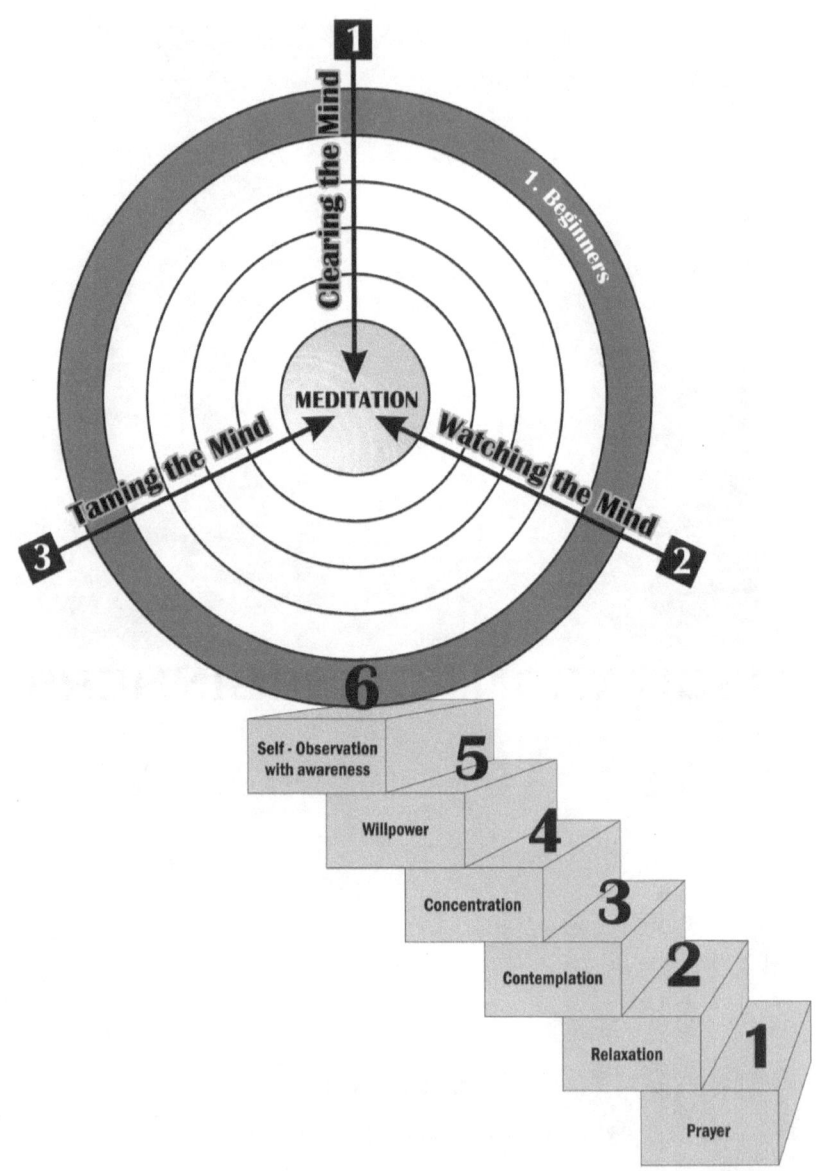

CHAPTER 1

What Is Meditation, What Is Not Meditation

Five Important Questions

Eliminating what you are not is meditation.

Awakening what you are is meditation.

Behaving as what you are not is unconsciousness.

Being and living as what you are is Supreme Consciousness.

This can be achieved through meditation on Supreme Consciousness.

Q. 1 : What is not meditation?

Sirshree :

1. Meditation is not attention.
2. Meditation is not concentration.
3. Meditation is not contemplation.
4. Meditation is not the techniques that are used for meditation.
5. Meditation is not separate or distinct from us.

The word 'meditation' has originated from spirituality. In India, spiritual seekers understood the deeper aspects of meditation. But today the word 'meditation' has become commonplace and is being used without an understanding of its deeper meaning. It has therefore lost its significance. In the Hindi language, the connotation of the word 'meditation' and the word 'attention' has become the same today, i.e. *dhyan*. *'Dhyan'* is nowadays commonly understood as attention, not as deep inner meditation. Likewise, in the English language too, the word 'meditation' has been synonymously used with 'reflection' or 'contemplation'. As a result, its deeper import has been lost.

Q. 2 : What is meditation?

Sirshree :

A. MEDITATION IS AN ATTRIBUTE

Actually meditation is an attribute of the Witness. The Witness which is called differently by different people – God, Allah, Self, Self-Awareness, Consciousness, etc. Meditation is that source within us which is awake even in deep sleep; it is self-awareness, which is present even in the state of unawareness.

B. MEDITATION IS THE PATH, MEDITATION ON THE SELF IS THE DESTINATION

The techniques designed to begin meditation or to improve concentration have also been known as 'meditation'. These so-called 'meditations' or concentration practices are a path to Self Meditation. Self Meditation means meditation on the 'Self' – the formless universal self, which is present everywhere and also within us. This is the real aim of meditation. Therefore, the word 'Self Meditation' is more appropriate than the word 'meditation.' Just improving concentration is not the goal of meditation. Concentration is a ladder in the path of meditation. Concentration improves with meditation. But if someone is meditating with the aim of improving concentration, then he is taking the least benefit of meditation. He has mistaken the means to be the end. Many a time it so happens that one begins on the path of meditation to attain Self Realisation, but gets content with improved concentration or some mystical powers. As a result, he strays away from his real goal. He wrongly believes some gains to be the goal.

C. MEDITATION IS AN ARROW

Meditation is such an arrow that can go either way, i.e. it can go towards the goal or towards the person with the goal. Meditation when turned outward can drift outside or can return within. This means that 'meditation' can meditate over the meditator.

D. MEDITATION IS WEALTH

Meditation raises man's level of consciousness. Due to this he is able to take the right decisions in life and is always happy by being the cause of happiness for others. This is why man, having attained the true wealth of meditation, never loses his high level of consciousness.

E. MEDITATION IS OUR RELIGION

Meditation is our actual religion. Just being a Hindu, Muslim, Sikh, Christian or Jew is not religion. To know our true nature and abide in it is religion. Meditation is our nature, our basic disposition. The true meaning of religion is our basic innate nature.

Q. 3 : What is wasted meditation (*vyavadhan*)?

Sirshree : The goal of meditation is to reach Self Meditation. But forgetting our original goal, we get caught up in enhancing our concentration, attaining powers, and activating the *kundalini* energy within us. Thus, instead of progressing from meditation to Self Meditation, we get stuck in wasted meditation (*vyavadhan*). *Vyavadhan* means hurdle or blockage. *Vyavadhan* means wasted meditation.

Q. 4 : How did meditation become *vyavadhan*?

Sirshree : Waves of desire arise in the mind. We then start judging what is good and what is bad. To quieten the thoughts and desires, the mind is given some anchor. For instance, in the ancient times, people used to chant the name of Lord Krishna or meditate on a visual form of God. Some would chant, some would practise penance, some would meditate, while some would practise such techniques that would be pleasing for the mind. Such techniques can be called meditation techniques. While practising these techniques, it is natural to experience a relaxed state of mind or joy. But people got so entangled in these techniques that they started believing that these techniques were the goal of meditation. Therefore, they were deprived from attaining Self Meditation. The reason being that those who were practising meditation lacked the insight or 'understanding', which is the vital missing link associated with meditation. Hence, meditation, which could have been a great help to reach the ultimate goal, became an obstacle in achieving Self Meditation.

On the path of meditation, one reaps immense rewards in physical, financial, professional as well as social life. One may get entangled in these benefits. One may then continue to work all his life on these techniques considering these gains to be his goal. Contrary to this, in spiritual life, the real aim is 'being aimless,' and that is attained through meditation.

Q. 5 : How were these techniques created?

Sirshree : Those who searched in depth (the realised ones like the Buddha, yogis and ascetics) understood that changes occur in breathing with every type of defilement (corruption) of the mind such as fear, anger, desire, lust, greed, etc. So they began to work on the breath. They took the support of breath as a tool for concentration and made it a technique for meditation. Some yogis made people practise body postures and breath regulation. These techniques were made for people in ancient times, and are difficult for the people in today's era. However, the same words, the same rituals and practices continue to be popular even today.

Due to this reason, people neither practise the ancient techniques, nor do they listen to anything new. The result is that those who can practise meditation become haughty with inflated egos. And those who are not able to do it develop a feeling of guilt in their minds as well as a fear of discontinuing meditation. In this way, due to lack of understanding, meditation makes the mind more egoistic and becomes an obstacle instead of leading to Self Meditation.

What happens in Self Meditation?
The Experiencer experiences the Experiencer
in the Experience.

CHAPTER 2

Necessities of Meditation

POSTURE, TIME, PLACE, MUDRA

Concentration is 'Exercise of the Mind'.
Meditation is 'Relaxation of the Mind'.
When the mind gets exhausted from working all day,
then just like the body, it too needs rest.
But when the mind just cannot sit quiet,
meditation provides tension-free relaxation.

Q. 6 : What is the importance of posture in meditation?

Sirshree : First let us see what is required to learn cycling. Some of the prerequisites are:

1. It should not be raining
2. Clothes should not be too tight or too loose
3. There should be a smooth open ground
4. The ground should not be slimy
5. There should not be a crowd, etc.

Only then can one learn to cycle easily. Similarly, for beginners of meditation, the posture, the *mudra*, the place, the time... all these aspects are important. Let us understand this in detail.

1. **ASANA (POSTURE)**

a. **Body posture :** Whenever the mind is restless, the body is hyperactive too and keeps moving. If the body stops moving, then the restless mind may also settle down. Therefore, for meditation, the posture should be such that the body remains steady. Choose *padmasan, sukhasan, vajrasan* or any such posture which is very convenient and comfortable, so that there is no tension in any part of the body. If there is tension in any part of the body, then consequently there can be tension in the mind too. Remember these two things while beginning meditation – don't meditate lying down or in the standing position. While lying down, there is a possibility of falling asleep and while standing you may soon get tired. Therefore, sitting is the best posture for meditation.

b. **The Seat :** For sitting, use a soft seat like a mattress, blanket, bedding or cushion. This would be comfortable for the body and the body will not feel tired soon and hence will be able to sit for a longer period of time.

c. **Position of Sitting :** While sitting, it should be ensured that the spine is straight, without tension, and makes a 90 degree angle with the ground. This is because when the spine makes a 90 degree angle with the ground, then it is straight and the resultant gravitational pull of the Earth on the body is minimal. Therefore, the body can sit in meditation for a longer period of time without tiring. Also, while standing, lying down or walking, keep the spine straight. Otherwise, the vertebral column becomes bent or crooked due to walking with a bent posture or due to a bent neck or waist. This reduces the confidence of the mind, induces laziness, has a dampening effect on the mind and therefore becomes an obstacle in meditation.

2. **MUDRAS (SYMBOLIC HAND GESTURES)**

Meditating in a particular mudra proves to be helpful. Several mudras have been mentioned, but the *Gyan Mudra* or Wisdom Posture is considered the best. This *mudra* is made by bringing the thumb and the index finger of the hand together, while the rest of the three fingers are kept straight. After making this *mudra*, keep both hands over the knees or on the lap, just like the 'Buddha Posture.'

There are reasons behind adopting these mudras. For example, when we go to the temple and join our hands to offer prayers, we feel the purity of the temple. Similarly, on adopting a mudra, the mind gets an auto-suggestion and agrees to calm down instantly.

Select a particular mudra and maintain this mudra every time you meditate for a continued and longer period of time. By giving yourself suggestions in that mudra, prepare the mind. After some practice, this mudra will be helpful in transferring you immediately into a meditative state wherever you are or whatever you are doing.

For instance, if somebody gives you some bad news, and you are not able to bear it, then at that juncture, adopt the mudra. You will find yourself transported to a state where you are calm, tension-free and relaxed, just as you are during meditation. Similarly, while facing an interview, while being on stage, while driving or while sitting on the backseat, this mudra will help you in boosting your self-confidence, concentration and memory.

3. TIME

The timings for meditation should not be such that it is sometimes at 6 a.m., at other times 9 a.m. or sometimes at night.

— It is essential to meditate at a particular fixed time.

— While meditating, the stomach should not be too full or too starved. Avoid both extremes.

— The proper time for meditation is the time around sunrise and sunset, which is the time of fusion. This is such a time when the stomach is neither full nor empty. Dinner is digested by morning and lunch is digested by evening. The atmosphere during the morning and evening is calm and cool. Due to this, even the mind becomes relaxed and pure much faster. In the beginning, for building concentration of the mind and reducing the instability of the mind, these considerations are extremely essential. When you fix up a particular time, it helps in concentrating better. If you perform a particular task at a particular time regularly, the mind becomes programmed for that task, and it stops running haphazardly.

— Early mornings are also recommended due to the fact that you are neither fully asleep nor fully awake at that early hour. This state is similar to the original state of our being.

4. PLACE

In meditation, the place is as important as the time.

- The room should be well ventilated. The environment in the room should be clean, calm, and quiet.

- There should not be any noise even in the surroundings of the room as noise interrupts the concentration of the mind. For example, if somebody outside is chattering on the subject of a picnic, the mind fancies listening to such topics of interest. The mind will wander to such a conversation again and again. But meditation is not for giving external pleasures to the mind; it is for making it quiet, focused and stable.

- If there is a telephone in the room, switch it off or disconnect it.

- Do not keep changing the place of meditation. Changing the place may disturb the concentration of the mind.

- A meditation room is not essential, but it is helpful if you have one. Otherwise, select any place or any corner of a room. And if you meditate every day regularly at the same place, on the same seat, in the same posture and at the same time, then you can reach the depths of meditation much sooner.

- Meditating in the woods is also helpful. The external Nature is helpful in knowing the internal nature.

Q. 7 : Once I have chosen the posture, time, place, and mudra, should I meditate with open or closed eyes? What about my breathing?

Sirshree :

Meditate with closed eyes: In the beginning, meditate with closed eyes until you have mastered the practice. With eyes open, there is a possibility of the mind getting entangled in external objects. If your eyes open again and again, you can sit facing the wall. Sit just a few inches from the wall. The wall should be blank without any pictures or patterns on it.

- Meditation can be done with the help of breath, pictures, words like 'Om,' repetition of a number, etc.

- For beginning meditation, watching the breath has been regarded as the best method. After this practice, you can meditate even while walking, sitting or standing.

- Breathing should be normal while meditating. There is a deep co-relation between the breath and the mind. Perhaps you may have noticed that whenever you are angry or your mind is upset, then the rate of breathing increases. When the mind is calm, the rate of breathing is low. When the breathing is slow, even the mind will begin to get calmer.

- If you want to meditate with open eyes, then you can practise by focusing on one spot or on a particular object, which is fixed and which is of no interest to the mind. With such meditation, the concentration power and inner strength increases.

- You can consider practising 'Group Meditation' by coming together in a group. While meditating in a group, if somebody begins to avoid the practice, then others can encourage and inspire him, remind and motivate him to meditate. A group can prove to be inspirational because the aim of all members is the same.

- **Continuity of meditation:** Meditation should be practised regularly and continuously. There should not be even a day's break, which can become the cause for laziness. Just like we take meals twice a day, we should meditate at least once or twice a day. As the continuity increases, meditation will become a part of you just like breathing. This is possible with constant practice. You will reap the benefits of this in the future.

– **Purity:** Physical purity has also been regarded as essential for meditation. Meditation after taking a bath and wearing clean and loose clothes is helpful.

Q. 8 : Any other essential instructions?

Sirshree: Other essential instructions are:

1. Do not be in a hurry to begin meditation. Carry out all the activities before meditation such as taking a bath, arranging a seat, etc. with patience. Every activity should be carried out in a slow, calm and committed manner. There is no need for impatience and haste.

2. It is more helpful if you have a spiritual master or a teacher because then you can share your experiences of meditation with him and receive guidance from him. If there is no such facility, then without paying attention to the physical experiences during meditation, you should continue practising meditation regularly.

3. For better results, plan your daily schedule. Avoid such activities which will create tension in the mind. If you can give up such activities, you may achieve results much faster.

4. A balanced and light diet is helpful in meditation.

5. There should be no hurry even after getting up from meditation. Get up and walk in a normal way. Let things happen on their own. Never try to hurry from your side.

6. To learn the meditation techniques in detail, you can listen to the audio tapes or CDs of the Meditation Retreat.

What you need to remember for meditation is :

1. Keep patience.
2. Develop your understanding.
3. Do not get stuck in the techniques.
4. Do not worry about the results and do not keep checking the results.

CHAPTER 3

What is Meditation

MEDITATION AND MIND

Whenever you have an option to do one out of two things, always choose to do something new.
For doing the usual, the mind is required.
For doing something new, awareness is required.

MEDITATION

Q. 9 : What is meditation? How do we understand it in a simple and easy manner?

Sirshree : A boy's father is displeased because his son is doing nothing. One fine day, the lad joins a meditation course. Now the father is very pleased and brags, "Now, my son, together with many other people, is doing 'nothing'."

The simple meaning of meditation is 'doing nothing'. But, for many people, even 'doing nothing' becomes very difficult. How to do nothing? It is like asking, "What should be done to get sleep faster?" The answer to this is, "You have to do nothing to get sleep, just go and lie down. If you are trying to get sleep, it will elude you. Otherwise, you can get sleep without doing anything quite easily." In the same way, meditation is a process in which there is no need to do anything; you only have to be.

Q. 10 : Why has meditation been given so much importance?

Sirshree : Meditation is also known as a yogic practice. Meditation (awareness) is necessary in every field of life. No work can be done without meditation. Meditation is essential for all activities of life. The body receives 'vibration of action' due to meditation. The instruments for all our activities are the five senses of our body – eyes, ears, nose, tongue and skin.

By senses, it is not meant the organs of perception, but rather their power of perception. The eye is not the sense, but the power of vision possessed by the eye is the sense. All five senses affect our body. Usually, when our senses are directed outward, they get involved in external objects and all the energy of our mind gets exhausted in those external matters. Therefore, it is necessary that we have some control over our senses. Meditation enables this.

Through meditation, it is possible to direct inwards the energy that is getting consumed in the external world. To shift the mind from external objects and stabilise it within is meditation.

MIND

Q. 11 : What is the mind?

Sirshree : Mind is only the medium of exchange of thoughts. Mind is a collection of many thoughts. Mind is a sack or bundle of thoughts. Thoughts is mind. If thoughts are sorrowful, then the mind seems to be distressed. If the thoughts are pleasant, then the mind becomes happy. The thoughts of the past and future are the food of mind on which it sustains. Intelligence is the tool of mind, which helps us in making decisions.

Q. 12 : What is the inner mind?

Sirshree : We have two minds within us. (This division has been made just for the sake of explanation). One is the conscious mind, also called as the external mind or simply the mind. The other is the subconscious mind, which is also called the inner mind, simple mind, intuitive mind or instinctive mind.

Q. 13 : What is the difference between the mind and the subconscious mind?

Sirshree : The difference between the mind and the subconscious mind is the same as the difference between the storm and the breeze. The work of the mind is visible, whereas the functioning of the subconscious mind is not visible. The subconscious mind works quietly, whereas the external mind experiences every activity, thought and emotion, and continuously makes assumptions. It just cannot sit quiet.

Q. 14 : Which is superior among the two?

Sirshree : Both minds are essential for functioning of the human body. Therefore, there is no question of one being better than the other. It is like asking, which one is superior between a flower and a fruit? The answer will be that both have their own definite functions, there is no question of superiority or comparison.

Q. 15 : What is the difference between Consciousness (Self), mind and subconscious mind?

Sirshree : The difference between Consciousness, mind and subconscious mind is that Consciousness regulates the mind; while the mind, by giving instructions, programmes the subconscious mind. At this junction, if we raise the question of superiority, then Consciousness is equivalent to the electricity lighting a bulb. There is no use of a bulb without electricity (the bulb here refers to the body-mind mechanism).

Q. 16 : Where is the mind?

Sirshree : Mind means a bundle of thoughts. On whatever your attention is directed, your mind starts thinking on that particular subject. If your attention goes on a garden, then the mind also gets transported there. In this way, the mind is where the attention is.

Q. 17 : Where is the inner mind?

Sirshree : The inner mind is not an object whose location can be specified. The inner or subconscious mind is made up of imagination, memory, intellect and the collective programming of the conscious mind.

Q. 18 : What is the function of each (the mind, the subconscious mind and the Consciousness)?

Sirshree : All three elements are required to operate this whole universe and to keep every living being functional in it. They are instruments created by God to carry out His divine play. As a dancer requires feet and other parts of the body for dancing, similarly varied dances (roles) are being performed by each and every one so that this play goes on smoothly. The aim of man is to 'know himself' through this drama and not get caught up in it or get identified with it.

Q. 19 : How does the mind get caught up?

Sirshree : Mind is such an organ which cannot be located in the body, but we have always accepted its presence. If somebody asks right now as to where is the mind, then the answer would be 'in the eyes' because we are now reading with our eyes. However, in the meantime, the mind went through the brain because it thought about this question. But it was so fast that we did not even realise it. The speed of mind is immense due to which we are not able to catch it. We can read and comprehend 200-300 words in a minute. But the speed of the mind is such that it can listen to 800 words in a minute. For this reason, the mind fills the gap for the remaining 500 words in the form of other thoughts. Consequently we are not able to concentrate the mind.

For the mind to become 'no mind' it is essential that first the number of our thoughts should reduce. Although the mind is able to grasp 800 words, it should be satisfied with just one or two words. That is why very often people take a word or a mantra for beginning meditation.

Do not meditate in order to show off.
Meditation is for annihilating the ego,
not for perpetuating the disease of ego.

CHAPTER 4

Twelve Benefits of Meditation

PHYSICAL, MENTAL, SPIRITUAL

Meditation is being natural and simple like a child – the child who sees things as a whole without labeling them. Whose eyes are innocent and whose words arise from the Experience of Being. That Experience which we have all experienced and happened to forget.

BENEFITS OF MEDITATION

1. Enhanced decision-making power
2. Breaking of attachment with thoughts and body
3. Increased sensitivity
4. Better control over feelings and emotions
5. More capacity to work
6. Improved concentration and memory
7. Present-mindedness
8. Awareness
9. Higher level of energy to work
10. Greater problem-solving power
11. Learning to experience the joy of silence
12. Complete relaxation and restoration of health of body and mind

PHYSICAL BENEFITS

Q. 20 : Does meditation cure physical ailments?

Sirshree : Every doctor advises the patient to take rest along with medicines. The reason being that 'rest' is that medicine which helps cure every ailment. But people do not know how to rest and relax. Thus, meditation is helpful and effective for every disease. Diseases such as asthma, high or low blood pressure, paralysis, etc. have been noted to improve with the practice of meditation. Meditation has definite positive effects on the mental and physical planes; though just better health is not the goal of meditation. In addition, meditation energises you, increases your capacity to live and work and helps in improving your physical vitality.

Q. 21 : How will my capacity increase with meditation?

Sirshree : Our capacity to work definitely increases with meditation. Some of the reasons are stated below:

A. The more the body can relax, the more it can work. And the more it works, the more capable it becomes. A calm mind can think in new directions and become creative. A creative mind has more capacity and only a relaxed mind can be creative. Hence a relaxed mind has so much importance in the technique of meditation. A relaxed mind is also beneficial for physical health. Diseases such as high blood pressure, heart disease, etc. are the result of stress. A healthy body possesses more capacity to work.

B. The concentration power of the mind increases with meditation. A concentrated mind alone can reach the depths of any subject. Concentration of mind is also essential for achieving anything in the external world. Even for reading, a focused mind is needed. With concentration, the memory power is strengthened and the distraction of mind and absent-mindedness is reduced.

C. Along with concentration, awareness is awakened. And because of awareness, the intellect becomes sharp. Achieving success in the external world thus becomes very easy. If the nervous system is tension-free, its capacity increases to the maximum and its efficiency is also enhanced. Success comes easily to such a person. Many such benefits are possible with meditation.

D. The scientific reason for increased capacity: It is the habit of the mind to get engrossed in the external world and exhaust itself. It gets tired fairly quickly because of its tendency to drain energy away. Meditation stops this drainage of energy and resultant fatigue, and thus the energy reserves in the body are enhanced. Mind has great powers. It is a great wonder in itself. Meditation is a medium to awaken the powers of the mind such as willpower, self-hypnotism, etc.

MENTAL BENEFITS

Q. 22 : Is meditation helpful in taking decisions?

Sirshree : A question that usually arises is: "What will I get by practising meditation?" But the question is: "What do you want from meditation?" What depths do you want to reach with meditation? Meditation can help you progress in every field of life.

If you are working on strengthening your willpower, then meditation can help you with that. You will be able to take your decisions on time as well as fulfil them. The reason for delay in taking decisions is 'attachment' with thoughts.

Q. 23 : So how can we break this attachment with thoughts?

Sirshree : Through meditation. Meditation is helpful in detaching you from attachment. Meditation gives you the ability of being detached from your thoughts. Thoughts become the hurdle that come between you and your decision and prevents you from making a decision. Meditation helps you think objectively by detaching you from thoughts. You are able to catch even the subtle or minutest of thoughts. This means your sensitivity increases and you can take decisions without getting attached to your thoughts.

Q. 24 : How will sensitivity increase with meditation?

Sirshree : You are always extremely sensitive about your possessions, your desires and your thoughts. You give more importance to thoughts. It is the thoughts that make you happy or unhappy. It is because of thoughts that you get angry or you become more egoistic. You see these thoughts coming under control through meditation. Then you are able to keep a restraint over your emotions and feel even the most subtle things. This very quality increases your sensitivity.

Q. 25 : What is meant by restraint over emotions?

Sirshree : Are you able to control yourself in minor and simple incidents? Can you walk away from a cricket match being played by your country? Can you give away your favourite object to others? Once you have taken a decision, are you able to fulfil it? How is your behaviour in stressful conditions? Are you able to bear any problem easily? Can you keep a restraint over yourself even during a fast? (Fasting is an exercise to increase self- restraint).

All this is possible through meditation. Besides concentration, even willpower increases with meditation. With increase in concentration, you can experience tranquility even amidst din and roar.

Q. 26 : Besides improved concentration, what are the other benefits of meditation?

Sirshree : Meditation also brings about a great change in your listening power. With constant meditation, you may be able to detect even those sounds which cannot be possibly detected by an ordinary person. You begin to perceive and understand those things which other people do not know. You begin to understand the depths of the mind. You begin to understand the games and tricks played by the mind. You are able to realise your mistakes, due to which you become cautious so as not to repeat them again in your life.

SPIRITUAL BENEFITS

Q. 27 : Is it possible to become present-minded with the technique of meditation?

Sirshree : Being present-minded is the first requirement of meditation. The technique of meditation is the technique of being in the present. If concentration is a torch, then meditation is a lantern. The light from a torch falls in one direction, while the light from a lantern spreads in all directions. With meditation, you are present in all your surroundings. Therefore, you are in the present, which means you are aware for your present. You are aware towards every event, every action and reaction. You are aware towards your thoughts. You are aware towards your presence, your being. You can attain this experience only in the present. Thoughts wander either in the future or in the past. And because of living in the past or the future, it becomes impossible to be in the present. Meditation teaches us to benefit from the present.

CHAPTER 5

Three Stages of Meditation

PURE MIND, QUIET MIND, NO MIND

Some people consider meditation as a 'waste of time.' But when they sleep for 7-10 hours, they forget to account for that time. The time given for meditation is not a waste, but an essential investment, without which we cannot work to our full capacity.

FIRST STAGE

Clearing the mind

Q. 28 : If meditation were to be divided into three main stages, then which is the stage that should be given first importance?

Sirshree : Clearing the mind should be given first importance. The mind is always entangled in thoughts. Either it keeps thinking about the future or wanders in the past. It never likes to stay in the present. In the first stage, we have to bring it from the multitude of negative thoughts towards positive thoughts. As far as possible, hatred and ill-will have to be removed from the mind. Forgiveness and tolerance should be practised. The mind should be purified by listening to the truth. The mind which harbours thoughts of well-being for others is good, pure and clear. Without purity of mind, if any powers are achieved, then the mind becomes egoistic instead of being subdued. Hence the mind should be pure and clear for beginning meditation. Then as the meditation evolves towards Self Meditation, it will be very easy to keep the mind pure. In the beginning, efforts will be required to fill the mind with kindness and compassion. In every sect, creed and religion of the world, purity of mind has been given importance. For example, the rules for control over the body and mind (*Yam-Niyam*), the five cardinal principles of life (*Panchsheel*), brotherhood, worship, prayer, etc., have been formulated for keeping the mind pure and peaceful.

Where negative thoughts end, 'Happy Thoughts' begin.

Where there are Happy Thoughts, the mind becomes pure.

Only a pure mind can bring about a thoughtless state.

And a thoughtless state takes us towards Self Realisation.

SECOND STAGE

Watching the mind

Q. 29 : What should be done after the mind becomes pure?

Sirshree : After the mind becomes pure, we have to know how to watch the mind and how to learn its behaviour. We cannot see the breeze, but through movement of the leaves, we can see its presence. Similarly, if you want to see the mind, then look at thoughts. Thoughts give the right information about the mind. In this stage, every thought has to be watched, without getting identified or lured by it. This is the most important stage. This is the stage where there are maximum chances of making mistakes. Also, it cannot be understood by watching the thoughts for the first time. Let us try to understand this with an example.

When we watch a movie or a programme on the television, initially we notice only a few aspects in it. When we see the same programme for the second time, the experience is different – we notice many more details. It is the same with the mind. When we watch a movie for the first time, our attention is focused totally on our favourite actor or actress. When we see it for the second time, then perhaps our attention may shift towards the people dancing or simply present in the background. Similarly, if we watch the mind again and again, we can discover the secrets of the mind. Each time, we would notice new aspects or get newer understanding. For the one who begins to understand the mind, life becomes easy. There will be peace, tranquility and harmony in his life.

THIRD STAGE

Taming the mind

Q. 30 : What is the last stage of meditation?

Sirshree : The last stage of meditation is – taming the mind. In this stage, you control your mind. Not forcefully, but with patience and understanding. But today it is seen that more often meditation is done forcefully. For example, it is our belief that when we are in a temple, we should not get negative thoughts or bad thoughts… 'I am a devotee of God, so I should be thinking only in this particular manner.' Similarly, when people practise meditation, they do so with preconceived ideas and notions.

We should go into meditation peacefully and in a relaxed manner with the thought: 'I don't know anything. Let me see what experience I get this time and what happens this time.' We should go ahead ignoring our past experiences because the mind always likes to hold on to old ideas. 'I have to see Lord Shiva, I have to see the divine light, I have to hear the divine music, I should be able to see God…' – we must keep all such imaginations, expectations and assumptions aside and meditate without any comparison with our previous experiences or that of others. A relaxed body will always be helpful for you. Understanding the thoughts will help you to be a master of your thoughts.

Just remember that 'I am meditating.' If, while meditating, you forget this and instead remember some work that you had to do and get caught up in those thoughts, then the mind is your master. You must always remember that you are meditating. You need to understand that the thoughts you are trying to banish are actually helping you by reminding you that you are not concentrating and that you are not fully aware. It is the thoughts which are indicating that your mind is somewhere else.

The most important thing to know is that, when you were without any thought, then who was it that told you that you were thoughtless? A thought came and told you, "You were thoughtless." Otherwise, until this thought came, how could you have known that thoughts had ceased! At this stage, we learn to make thoughts an instrument to help us achieve our goal. After this, the mind will start behaving like a good servant, it will be a 'no-mind.'

Just One Word

A king asked a sage, "For the benefit of all, please tell me in one sentence what is the essence of religion?"

The sage replied, "I will tell you in one word."

The king said, "Please, tell me that word."

"Silence."

"How to attain silence?"

"By meditating."

"How should we meditate?"

"By being Silence."

CHAPTER 6

Six Steps of Meditation

THE POWER OF THE SUBDUED, FOCUSED AND AWARE MIND

Does a non-believer have to become a believer before meditation? Not at all. Because even a non-believer cannot doubt his own existence. Very soon he will start believing in God and doubting himself. Thus a great believer will be born. "Only God exists; find out and confirm whether you exist..."

STEP 1

PRAYER

Q. 31 : Can prayer be used in meditation?

Sirshree : Let us understand about prayer in detail.

THE POWER OF PRAYER

The feeling of prayer is extremely beneficial for beginning meditation. Being in a prayerful state at the beginning of meditation is indeed very helpful. Prayer is the greatest power in the world, which has been given to man as a solution even before a problem arrives. By not using a superpower like prayer and only believing in their ego, many are being very foolish. Prayer has tremendous power. Prayer can cool down the pyre of worry and turn a stone into wax. It can placate a storm and bring a sinking ship to safe shores. Not only can desires be fulfilled with prayers, even ultimate liberation or *moksh* can be attained with prayer. Hand over all your problems and worries to God. Then imagine that God has solved them in an appropriate manner. This step will send your prayer and your thoughts to every nook and corner of the universe and pave the way for the fulfillment of your desire. That is why prayer is even more important than the meditation technique and it should certainly be done before starting a sacred practice like meditation. It will prove beneficial for you in the process of meditation.

WHAT AND HOW TO PRAY

Repeat the words given below slowly, lovingly, in good rhythm, with deep feeling and complete faith. These words have tremendous power to relax your mind. Let the first step be right. Well begun is half done. Therefore, learn this prayer by heart and take the first step.

> "I am peaceful in the presence of God (Silence).
>
> I am experiencing complete peace.
>
> I am created by God.

> Therefore, tranquility, peace, happiness,
> which is the nature of God,
> is spreading within my heart and mind.
> God has created nothing to disrupt this peace.
> Whatever may be the reason of my turmoil,
> it is not in the list of the Almighty.
> I am offering myself in his lap just like
> a tired child rests in the lap of his mother.
> Waves of joy are arising all around me and
> I am feeling a sense of peace everywhere.
> Peace... Peace... Peace..."

WHAT NEEDS TO BE DONE DURING PRAYER

In prayer, one should always use positive words and words that are full of devotion. Words are important in a prayer because certain words enhance the devotional feeling within us, touch us, make us aware, and inspire us. Some words are such that by simply listening to them, we can feel that ecstatic feeling within us. Prayer should always be done with faith and a feeling of love.

Prayer is done before meditation, which helps in entering the meditative state. And when we have completely reached and stabilised in that meditative state, the greatest prayer begins. Only when we are actually absorbed in meditation, it is then that the prayer begins. There are no words in that prayer. The body that has completely reached that meditative state is totally receptive and therefore there can be no higher prayer for it than the disappearance of the individual ego and the elimination of the apparently separate individual. Just his being is the greatest prayer. This prayer will create many more things.

POSTURE DURING PRAYER

When we pray with hands joined together, bow down or sit in a particular posture, all these are helpful in prayer. These are indications or signs for the ultimate wisdom that God should work through our body. Such a person receives God's help through prayer. God is unable to help a person who is haughty and egoistic. The more egoistic a man is, the lesser can God express through him, and therefore expression of the individual ego becomes more prominent.

BEGINNING OF MEDITATION

Prayer, when done before beginning meditation, helps create feelings that ease the process of entering the state of meditation. And when you are completely absorbed in meditation, real prayer begins. You begin to achieve the aim that you wanted to attain through meditation. This implies that prayer and meditation are both one and the same. If you think from the starting point of view, then the beginning is made with prayer and it ends in meditation.

100% PRAYER

The power of prayer is very helpful to get into the depths of meditation. But this requires your 100% involvement and participation in prayer. You should completely immerse yourself in prayer with full feeling. The more the feeling you can put into your prayer, the better it will be. Before commencing with the prayer and meditation, say to yourself, "I will pray with 100% feeling and participate completely." And then begin the prayer. You may pray loudly if you wish, you may sing or even raise your hands to pray. After completing the prayer, just relax and be calm. Then tell yourself, "I am receptive for the truth, I am receptive for grace. I am open to receive the grace of meditation being showered upon me." If you sit in this receptive state, you will automatically go into the depths of meditation.

Collective Meditation and Prayer

Very little is known in science about the power of prayer. Even today people do not have much knowledge about the power of prayer. If all the people of the world get together to meditate at the same place and the same time, the level of consciousness of the entire world can be raised at once. When each and every one in this world prays together for just two minutes for the problems that the whole world is facing, then this two-minute prayer will bring about such tremendous results which simply cannot be imagined. One prayer can put to end all the problems of the universe.

When many people pray collectively at the same time, that prayer has enormous power. The concentrated thoughts and feelings of everyone can eradicate violence, poverty, natural disasters and sufferings or problems of all kinds from the world.

In the religious scriptures, God has spoken thus: "O Narada! I do not dwell in the heavenly abode nor do I dwell in the hearts of ascetics, I dwell where my devotees gather together to sing my praises and pray."

Such collective prayer has incredible magnetism. It has strong vibrations of collective strength, collective power, collective relationship, and collective feeling. These vibrations go on increasing and strengthening till they finally saturate the entire atmosphere with those feelings. In such an atmosphere, the feelings of discrimination, evil and immoral habits and desires, and atheism are uprooted. All negative energies are replaced by the rise of feelings of brotherhood, oneness, love, devotion, unity, equality and complete faith.

This custom is largely prevalent in almost all religions, in which people pray together with others and also for others; this in turn purifies the mind. A pure and pious mind easily gets ready to bend down and dissolve. It is only after the mind dissolves that Self Realisation takes place.

PRAY WITH AWARENESS

Prayer is power. In fact, we can say that prayer is the greatest power. Now it depends on us how we are using this power and for what purpose. For example, fire is an energy. We can use it to protect ourselves from the chilly winters or to cook food or to burn down someone's house. The same applies to prayer. Prayer is like Aladdin's magic lamp. If a genie appears before you and asks you what is your desire, what will you say?

If you are praying with awareness, only then can you ask for the right things. When there is no awareness, you may ask for rather trivial or insignificant wishes to be granted when you could have had something really big. If someone were making an elephant pick up a matchstick, what would you tell such a person? You would probably say, "What are you doing? Recognise the strength of an elephant. It can even uproot a huge tree. You are asking for too little." If this awareness were awakened in him, he would never commit this mistake while asking for favours to be granted in prayer.

We too should examine ourselves as to what requests we are making, and what we can get. Are we asking for very less? If we grow in wisdom, only then we will be able to pray for the right thing. When the power of prayer is not known, all the favours requested are very small. People keep praying that I should get rid of my worldly problems, I should win a jackpot, I should get rid of my sickness, I should get a good job, my project should get completed, and so on.

The person who is aware will request for the ultimate. He will pray for reaching the depths of meditation, he will pray for getting stabilised in the state of Samadhi – the last and highest level of meditation. He will pray for attaining liberation from the bondages of this material world, from false beliefs, from illusion, from anger, from his deeds, from ego. (He knows that by asking for worldly pleasures, he will never derive the complete benefit of his birth as a human being). But these desires can be fulfilled only when he raises his level of understanding. Otherwise in his ignorance he will believe this illusory world to be the reality and his worldly success to be true success. Hence the first thing that you should do is to recognise the importance of prayer. First pray to know the importance of prayer. This prayer is the prayer before prayer, it is *Tej* prayer.

If one is praying for his bright future, he does not know that through prayer he can get freedom from both at the same time – the burdens of the past as well as worries of the future. When one prays to get rid of sickness, he is unaware that with the power of prayer he can be liberated from the cycle of life and death. One is praying for success in exams and for acquiring a lot of knowledge which is actually (information), but he forgets that by true prayer, he can learn the secret of the universe.

In this way man keeps asking for something or the other. But one day it will dawn upon him that he has done many things, but has not done that thing for which he was born on Earth. He will always regret it. He had prayed a lot for a long life, but never for the wisdom of how to live life. He had prayed to get good friends or to meet his relatives, but if he had prayed for a true spiritual master (*Tejguru*), the master would have made him understand the true meaning of relationships. The advent of the Tejguru in his life could have been the greatest blessing for him. Liberation is possible in this very life. Then why shouldn't you ask for it, why should you ask for anything less?

Awareness increases with understanding. Whenever we increase our understanding about something, it leads to awakening of our awareness. If, with awareness, we make the proper use of intellect and request for that which lies beyond the intellect, then the prayer for grace is the greatest of all prayers.

In all religions and all sects, the importance of prayer has been emphasised. Many people do pray regularly. In fact many people pray all their lives from childhood to old age. But, before praying, man should contemplate on, 'What do I want to ask? And what I am asking for, is it the right thing?'

In some homes, people follow the custom of prayer at a particular time. Due to this custom, even the children in that home begin to pray, and after growing up they teach the same to their children. It may so happen that after some generations the true meaning of prayer is lost and we just continue to repeat prayers mechanically without any awareness. The time of the prayer and the words used were according to the need of that time, but are we perhaps offering the same prayer mechanically and unconsciously, without thinking what are we praying for and why?

STEP 2

Relaxation

Q. 32 : What should be done to relax the body in meditation?

Sirshree : For relaxation, *pranayam* (breath regulation) can also be used. For example, inhaling (breathing in) at the count of 4 and exhaling (breathing out) at the count of 6. In this way, breathing is controlled. This is beneficial for health as well as relaxation. Pranayam is useful in balancing the level of oxygen in the body and is also effective in eliminating carbon dioxide from the body.

Besides pranayam, the following technique is also helpful for relaxation:

– In the sitting or lying down position, take a deep breath and release it slowly.

– To relax your mind, you can visualise one such natural scene which has been dearest to you. For example, the scene of a beautiful garden or a beach or a natural waterfall cascading down a mountain where you had been for a picnic.

– Let your eyes wander in that scene. Pay attention to all the important details in that scene.

– When your mind has seen and experienced the complete scene, then check your body. If there is still some tension in some part of the body, contract that part and then let it loose again. Then instruct that part: "Release the tension... relax... relax... relax..." In this way release the tension from the arms, legs, shoulders, back, knees and eyes. This technique is effective for relaxation of the body.

STEP 3

CONTEMPLATION

Q. 33 : What is the importance of contemplation in meditation?

Sirshree : To know a subject in depth and to understand it completely requires 'contemplation.' For example, if you are told, "Think about a pen," you do think on it for some time and then your thinking stops. But contemplation means thinking even after that. At that moment, you have to think only about a pen and on no other subject. Along with contemplation comes brooding (counter contemplation). There is a big difference between the two. Contemplation means thinking initially about the positive aspects and later on the negative aspects. Counter contemplation is the complete opposite, in which case a person thinks first on the negative aspects and then on the positive aspects. For instance, if somebody sees a bush of roses and if he is going to contemplate on it, his attention would be first drawn towards the beauty of the flowers and then he will also realise the importance of the thorns that these thorns are for protection of the flowers. But if he is going to counter contemplate on the subject, then right in the beginning his attention will be drawn towards the thorns and he would not be able to appreciate the beauty of the flowers. He would thus be deprived from experiencing the joy of nature. That is why contemplation has been given importance and not counter contemplation.

'Contemplation' is a technique for focusing the mind. Contemplation is the technique of choice for intellectuals who want to focus their mind. Some things, which are not easy to understand, can be understood through contemplation. In fact, without contemplation, even diamonds are just pieces of carbon. (This means that you would not realise the value of even priceless spiritual knowledge you have gained until you contemplate upon it; it may remain as mere information with you).

Contemplate on the following points and develop your power of discrimination (*viveka*):

1. How was your face before you were born?

2. How was your face before your parents were born? (If you keep thinking over this, initially you will get the wrong answers, but later on you may get the right answers).

3. Every person should keep taking some calculated risks. This will result in progress and one will definitely move ahead.

4. Instead of not taking any decision, it is better to take a wrong decision and learn something from it. Those who took wrong decisions, gained the experience, and learnt the art of making right decisions. Experience increases with taking wrong decisions and consequently teaches how to take the right decisions.

5. Death is a long sleep, and sleep is a short death. Do not die before dying. You should die only once in your life rather than dying every day due to fear.

6. The strength to fight problems has been given to us even before the problems arise. Even before a child is born, the arrangement for its milk is already made by nature.

7. Every bad person also has some virtues in him. They must be certainly getting the reward for these virtues too.

8. The one who is liberated from luck is lucky. God (Consciousness) is present within everyone; then who is the one who is not lucky?

9. Sorrow does not appear in your life to make you unhappy. Sorrow comes to wake you up.

10. Just the presence of desire is not the cause of sorrow. Identification of the mind with that desire is the cause of sorrow.

STEP 4

Concentration

Q. 34 : What is the exercise for the mind?

Sirshree : Concentration is exercise for the mind – the mind which is heavy and dull. When the mind is full of thoughts, then that mind is heavy and dull. Such a mind is not sensitive. It cannot go into the depths of a subject. This mind will have to be made sharp, active and sensitive. It will have to be trained in concentration. Concentration is not the goal, but concentration can be instrumental in achieving the goal. Concentration signifies focusing the mind on one particular point to the exclusion of everything else. This is something which the mind does not like at all. During the practice of concentration, three possibilities can occur with the mind:

1. The mind gets bored with concentration.

2. During concentration, a state of no-mind results.

3. With concentration, the mind becomes ready for working in depth.

Besides the above :

– In the practice of concentration, initially the mind will get bored, sleepy or make excuses. But very soon it will get ready to reach the depth of meditation.

– Every day, work on such a technique of meditation that will help increase your concentration.

STEP 5

WILLPOWER

Q. 35 : How can we increase our willpower for meditation?

Sirshree : Mind is a good servant, but a very bad master. We all have a wild and crazy mind. It is necessary to control it and be its boss. But how? Mind is like a desirous snake. It is filled with desires. On fulfillment of one desire, it jumps to another. Hence, as soon as a desire arises, do not immediately get down to fulfilling it. Consult your intellect on this and accordingly halt that desire for some time and then fulfil it or totally give up that desire. (You can certainly experiment this with some desires).

In the beginning, a gap of some time in fulfilling a desire is helpful. Your control over your mind will start increasing. Even halting your desire for some time will help build your self-confidence and willpower. With some practice, you will no longer remain a slave of your mind; instead these desires will then become the medium for strengthening your willpower.

In everyday life, many people make some resolutions, but are not able to fulfil them. Therefore, it is imperative to change this habit of the mind. It can be changed through some small experiments. For example:

1. You are eating and your plate contains two pieces of your favourite cake. You have already eaten one piece. Leave the other piece in the plate and walk away, even though the cake is very delicious and tempting.

2. You are watching a very interesting programme or your favourite sport on the television. Leave it halfway and walk out of the room.

3. Somebody gave you some good news. Instead of jumping with joy, listen to it calmly and thank the person.

4. When you feel like giving advice even when not asked for, hold it immediately.
5. If you feel tempted to pull somebody's leg or pass a comment or make fun of someone, restrain yourself at once.
6. Before going to bed at night, ask yourself, "Is there one more thing that I can do?" and do it. This is a good technique to develop your willpower.
7. To boost your willpower and to overcome your laziness, carry out one or two new tasks today which you feel are not necessary or can be postponed to tomorrow.
8. To challenge your fear, speak to a stranger. Accept an invitation to deliver a speech. The mind will find it uncomfortable but this challenge will do wonders for your confidence and your willpower.
9. Take up the responsibility of organising an event. Try being the organiser of a seminar. This is a good opportunity to challenge your willpower.

The above were some examples (you can choose some from these) which can help strengthen your willpower.

STEP 6

Self-observation with awareness

Q. 36 : How can we make our mind deceit-free?

Sirshree : Through self-observation, when the mind begins to see the truth and understand that the cause of its misery is deceit, then it becomes ready for becoming deceit-free.

Self-observation means observing oneself in every occurrence, event or happening. You can try doing the following experiment. After every hour, ask yourself what is your present state of mind. From the states given below, what is the state of your mind:

A – anger: On yourself or on others.

B – boredom: Dejection, having no interest in anything.

C – confusion: Inability to understand even after trying.

D – depression: Feeling sad and hopeless with or without reason.

E – ego: Haughty, arrogant, taking credit, self-praise.

F – fear: Fear that something untoward may occur or some nervous foreboding.

G – guilt: Blaming oneself with the feeling, 'Why did I do this?'

H – happiness: A state of joy.

I – ill-will: Feeling of hostility, enmity, malice or desire to hurt others.

J – jealous: Envious, resentful, unsteady, ambitious mind with the feeling, 'If he has this particular thing, why don't I?'

K – kindness: Sympathy, compassion, feeling of being helpful and caring for the goodwill of others.

L – lazy: Indolent, lethargic. Not feeling like doing anything. Prominence of laziness. Dull mind.

In this way, try and check the state of your mind every hour of the day, by asking yourself the question, 'What is the present state of my mind?' Your self-inspection will become your self-examination. Your awareness will increase and the birth of the Self Witness will occur. The desires and the state of mind keeps on changing constantly. Restlessness is its nature. Observe your mind. You will see that sometimes the mind will be agitated and sometimes it will be happy. Sometimes it is full of anger, at other times it is tainted with greed. Sometimes it is scared and fearful and at other times it is worried and frustrated. Sometimes it is filled with hatred and sometimes with guilt. Sometimes egoistic and at other times full of desires and longings. Sometimes devious and sometimes logical.

Sometimes comparing and judging, sometimes lost in imagination. Sometimes unaware, sometimes aware.

This hourly self-examination will create miracles. Very soon you will begin to understand the mind, not with the intellect but with your own experience, that the mind is an illusion. It can never remain in one state. If this is how the mind is, then why do we get identified with it? This insight will dawn upon you. If the mind is upset, then I am not upset. This clarity will arise. Then this experience will reflect in your life.

Any thought of joy or sorrow will not be able to displace you from your centre. 'It is the mind alone that is distressed, and it is the mind that is happy. Anger, hatred, guilt, fear... everything is with the mind, not with me' – this realisation will arise. The understanding will emerge that despite the ever-changing mind, it makes no difference in my bright happiness. Then even during tension and stress, you will be able to remain calm (from inside). 'This stress is for my mind and body and not for me.' You will understand that this stress or tension has appeared to get some work done through your body, just like tension before examinations is necessary for a student so as to motivate him to study. With this type of self-observation, you would know how you are at any given moment. Whether you are good or bad is not important, the important thing is that you have become ready to see yourself honestly.

Ignorance is the disease,
Understanding is the remedy.
Unconsciousness is the problem,
Self Meditation is the solution.

CHAPTER 7

How to Meditate

THOUGHTS, SLEEP, DREAMS

Every work in this world is done with the help of the mind. Meditation is the only thing which happens when there is no mind.

Q. 37 : How should we meditate? (How will the mind become ready to bow down)?

Sirshree : Today if your mind is an obstacle for you, tomorrow the same mind can become your biggest asset. It only needs to receive understanding – the understanding that it is standing in front of the idol of the truth (inner bliss) and blocking it from our view. Then it may get ready to bow down and become the cause for bliss. The mind is like the secretary who wants to go in the boss's cabin to check what he is doing so that she can let you in. But whenever she goes in, she finds the boss sleeping. The day she comes to know that it is her perfume that sedates the boss, she will stop going in. Once she gets this understanding, there is no need for her to know anything else. You can then meet the boss (the truth) directly.

Q. 38 : What needs to be specifically done in meditation?

Sirshree : Practising meditation means 'doing nothing', i.e. being thoughtless. Meditation begins with awareness, where for the first time we begin to know our thoughts. The reason for not knowing our thoughts is that we are identified in such a way with our thoughts that our morning (beginning) is with thoughts and our night (end) is also with thoughts. These include thoughts of joy, sorrow, depression, restlessness, over-enthusiasm, worry, agitation, and so on. It is as if we have given our remote control in the hands of thoughts. When we are able to know these thoughts with awareness, we attain a state where there are no thoughts – a thoughtless state. It is when we reach this state that we are in meditation. First we have to attain purity of mind, followed by a quiet mind. Only then does the no-mind state ensue.

SLEEP AND THOUGHTLESSNESS

Q. 39 : Is it possible to stay in a thoughtless state and for how long?

Sirshree : The other day a question was asked to seekers, "How much time in a day can we remain in a thoughtless state?" Various answers came from various people such as 1 minute, 2 minutes, 5 minutes, 15 minutes, a few seconds, etc. But the actual answer is shocking. We can remain in a thoughtless state for six to eight hours a day! Initially, people could not believe it. But when they heard that we remain in a thoughtless state in sleep, then they saw the reality. It is a fact that every one of us remains in a thoughtless state for six to eight hours and this is our most natural and favourite state. That is why everybody wants to go into sleep, and we feel restless and unwell if we are unable to get sleep.

Q. 40 : Why do we like sleep so much?

Sirshree : When we are in a thoughtless state in sleep, we forget everything. We forget our name, our profession and even our body. We forget our fatigue as well as all our physical and mental problems. Whatever the intensity of our sufferings, we forget all our difficulties and worries in sleep.

We forget the whole world in sleep; the only reason is 'thoughtlessness.' There are no thoughts in sleep. On waking up in the morning, the 'I' thought arises and in an instant the whole world appears before us – the same 'I', the same name, the same house, the same relatives, the same everything. A moment back there was nothing and the next moment the world of thoughts emerges. Due to the 'I' thought, the entire world emerges in a flash.

Q. 41 : Then why don't we get sleep immediately?

Sirshree : Whenever we lie down for sleep, thoughts still continue in our mind. Thoughts of the day's work or thoughts of tomorrow are constantly on. Our entire past passes through our mind or the train of imaginary thoughts of our future goes on. And then comes a time when we drift into sleep. Drifting into sleep means cessation of all thoughts. Until thoughts are going on, there can be no sleep.

One moment back the thoughts we had, our activities, our sufferings, our worries, our problems, everything disappears the very next moment as if they never existed. In an instant, we forget the whole world; we never remember the last thought we had before sleep. There is only one method to forget the world altogether and that is by being 'thoughtless'.

Q. 42 : What is our relation with thoughts, sleep and time?

Sirshree : Does this physical world, which appears and disappears in a moment, really exist? Or is it merely a game of thoughts? In other words, when there are thoughts, there is the world. When there are no thoughts, there is no world. Then all the people, the houses, the scenes, the trees, the animals, the objects – are all these real or do they merely exist in thoughts? Or is all this, this whole world, just a thought, of which we too are a part? Then are we too merely a 'thought'?! Is our life just a 'series of thoughts'?

If we observe carefully, we find that we don't even realise how fast time passes by when we are in a thoughtless state. We sleep all night, yet we feel as if we have slept only for a few minutes. How much time has then actually passed? We feel, 'I slept just a while ago and it is already morning!' This is because we do not get the thought of time in sleep. But when we are doing something which we consider uninteresting or when we are waiting for something or somebody, even five minutes seem to be a long time. If we work for ten hours in a day, we can tell for how much time we have worked because at that time thoughts are going on, which look at the clock and tell us the amount of time that has passed. But there is no sense of time in sleep. When we are involved in our favourite activity, hours slip by and we do not even realise it because we are lost in that work and we are intermittently in a thoughtless state. This implies that when there are thoughts, there is time. When there are no thoughts, there is no time. So, does time really exist, or is it also just a thought?

Q. 43 : Then how can we achieve a state of thoughtlessness?

Sirshree : There are many techniques to become thoughtless, some of which are stated below:

- Some people focus the mind, which means from many thoughts they come to focus on one thought and then suddenly become thoughtless.
- Some work on breathing techniques.
- Some chant a spiritual mantra (*japa*) while others chant the name of God (*naam smaran*).
- Some people work on thoughts, i.e. they watch their thoughts.

But underlying all these thoughts, one thought always remains constant, and that is: 'I have to become thoughtless.' This is also a thought. As long as it is present, we cannot be thoughtless. If somebody asks you, what do you do to get sleep, then your answer may be that you lie down and close your eyes. But actually, when all activities cease, it is then that you get sleep; even thinking ceases. Hence, we should not even intend that thoughts should stop appearing. Only then we will be able to achieve a thoughtless state.

Q. 44 : What if we get thoughts even in sleep?

Sirshree : If thoughts stop arising, then that is the state of sleep, and if thoughts arise in sleep, then these thoughts get converted into dreams. Dreams are a form of thoughts. That is why everything going on in a dream feels real. We get lost in the dream, which is unreal, but we feel as if it is real. When we wake up, we realise that it was only a dream which breaks as soon as it is morning. The dream has no effect on us at all. Dreams are just a play of thoughts.

If we think deeply, then what happens with us every night? We forget all about the world and we are transported to a different plane. Then is it that during the day too a dream is going on… a dream that is broken every night and starts again every morning at the same place where it had stopped the previous night?

DREAMS AND THOUGHTS

Q. 45 : If that is so, then what is the difference between the dream of the day and the dream of the night?

Sirshree : The only difference between the dream of the day and the dream of the night is that we get different dreams every night, while we get the same dream every day. If we see the difference between sleep and wakeful state, then we will realise that there are no thoughts during sleep and there are thoughts in the wakeful state. If there are thoughts, it signifies that the 'mind' is present. Mind is called the 'flow of thoughts'. At night, we go to sleep. That means our thoughts go to sleep. When thoughts go to sleep, it means the mind has gone to sleep. Then everything that happens due to thoughts ceases. And in the morning, as soon as a thought arises, the mind comes back. With this the world begins... everything begins. Then it can be said that at night the mind sleeps and in the morning the mind wakes up.

When we awaken from sleep in the morning, we say, "I slept." But if I was sleeping, then who is this 'I' who was perceiving that I was sleeping? This means that the one who was awake the whole day was awake even during the night... the one who has never ever slept till date; the one who is seeing two dreams, one of the night and one of the day.

Q. 46 : Who is that?

Sirshree : That is the actual *you* – who has seen every occurrence till today with awareness; who is seeing both types of dreams while remaining separate, who does not get lost in these dreams... who is beyond duality, beyond polarities... who is beyond thoughts... who is the Witness, the Self Witness.

Q. 47 : Then, do we have to try to stop our thoughts?

Sirshree : Definitely not. This does not mean that we have to try to stop our thoughts or fight with thoughts to drive them away. We only have to know thoughts. And this is possible through meditation. For this, we will have to know from where thoughts arise. When we find out the original source of thoughts, we will be able to benefit from thoughts. It is important to know the ocean from which the 'wave of thought' arises. And meditation helps us to know that ocean. Meditation is a technique to go into those depths.

Q. 48 : How can we reduce the number of thoughts?

Sirshree : There is no need for you to do anything. Just know that you are the knower. When you are not the thoughts, then why do you fight thoughts? We get identified with the thoughts and feel that we are the thoughts. Once you have the conviction that 'I am not the thoughts', then it does not matter how many waves are there in the ocean; you can always take a dip. You don't have to wait for the waves to stop. You don't have to think, 'Let these waves stop. Then I will take a dip.' Otherwise, all your life you will remain standing on the shore. You will never be able to take a dive in the depth of the ocean.

MEDITATION AND BLANKNESS

Q. 49 : What is blankness in meditation?

Sirshree : You are watching a video. You notice that for some time no picture can be seen, only the white screen is visible. What do you say then? That you became blank or the picture became blank? The white screen is called blankness. Similarly, when we become thoughtless (pictureless), we say that I became blank.

This is a great misunderstanding, a false belief, an illusion that when our thoughts cease, 'we' become blank. It is an old habit of the mind that it always wants answers in words. If somebody is meditating on 'Who am I?' and no answer comes forth, then the mind feels there is no answer. But the answer to this question is not in words.

Q. 50 : When we are meditating on 'Who am I' (self-enquiry), we experience blankness. Does that have any special meaning?

Sirshree : Who is that who is feeling the blankness? It is important to understand this. Who became blank? If the blankness resulted in an obstacle in meditation, then you did not progress further. If that blankness takes you onto yourself – on the real you – then it has more value. (For learning in detail about the 'Who am I' or self enquiry meditation, read Chapter 16).

HOW TO MEDITATE

Q. 51 : Is it necessary to meditate even after the mind becomes completely focused?

Sirshree : Let us understand the answer to this question through an example. A small child has fear of darkness. Therefore he avoids a lot of things and runs away from them. So his mother gives him a talisman. It is a lucky charm that is supposed to ward off evil and provide protection. After wearing that talisman, the boy has become a bit courageous. He goes about on his own and is also able to take decisions on his own. Then he grows up. But even then he is clinging on to the talisman. His mother tells him, "Son, remove it. Now you have grown up and you don't need it anymore." But the son is not ready to remove it. He feels that even today he needs it. His mother had given him the lucky charm for other reasons... such as he should become fearless, courageous and self-confident; he should be able to face darkness and go out boldly in a crowd. This charm was helpful for development of these qualities in his childhood. But after achieving those qualities, he has absolutely no need to carry it around with him.

In the same manner, the goal of meditation is to lead you to Self Meditation. If you reach there, then leave it. When you cross the river in a boat, then you leave the boat; you don't take it along with you. Similarly, after achieving your goal, there is no need to practise meditation because *you* have become meditation. You will realise that meditation is your attribute, your intrinsic nature.

Q. 52 : Is it necessary to renounce the world and practise meditation (practise austerities)?

Sirshree : It is a false belief that those who go into spirituality need to leave their homes and cut off their associations with all people and society, and become a recluse. Here, it is told that your aim is to become a Bright man of the world... a complete man. One who is beyond both, renouncing and enjoying the material world. One who is happy wherever he is and gives happiness to others. And whatever he does, he does it easily and effortlessly. He does not consider any difficulty to be a problem. There is no need to renounce anything. With meditation, whatever is unnecessary is cast off spontaneously. There arises no need to renounce anything.

Q. 53 : Then actually how should meditation be done?

Sirshree : You cannot do meditation. You can only prepare for it. You can only show your receptivity through your patience and persistence. Let us understand this in detail. When you want to sleep, what do you do? Is sleep under your control that you can sleep whenever you want to? No. You only show your readiness for sleeping by:

- wearing loose clothes
- putting off the lights
- lying down on the bed
- closing your eyes, etc.

On doing all the above, you don't get sleep. But all this is an indication, a readiness, a need expressed by you. If you try to bring sleep, then it will be all the more difficult to get sleep. Effort is the enemy of sleep because sleep is being free from every effort. In the same manner, meditation is also an awakened sleep. You cannot achieve it through any effort. You can only prepare for it.

Concentrating the mind is a part of the preparation. Place, posture, relaxation, bath, aroma, chanting, etc. are just some requirements for meditation. Eligibility and readiness to have patience and courage only increase the possibility of you entering the state of meditation. But your biggest preparation is 'understanding the truth.' Thus, if your preparation is complete, then meditation will happen effortlessly and you will attain the wealth of meditation. You will find that place within you (*tejasthan*) where there is silence, bliss, love... the place where fear, worry and stress simply cannot reach. To get stabilised in that place is the goal of every technique and every preparation.

Taking refuge in that place whenever any unhappy situation arises in life and getting relief from it is the reward of meditation, the gift from meditation.

Always be patient and have a positive attitude. Use the technique, but don't get entangled in the technique. Do not worry about the results, nor check the results. Because the mind will never be able to perceive that experience, just like the spectacles can never see the eyes. The mind should hence meditate with a feeling of surrender and acceptance.

When you are in front of a mirror,

you see your own self.

You are the object which is seen as well as you are the subject or the seer.

This means the seer and the seen are one.

This is what happens in meditation,

but it happens within.

CHAPTER 8
Questions on Meditation
MISCONCEPTIONS ABOUT MEDITATION

People have added many of their own wrong beliefs and notions with meditation because of which the technique of meditation itself has become more important. The false beliefs and notions which stick to the mind, then become dirt and grime, and spread their stench, destroying happiness. 'Meditation' is cleaning of the dirt so that we again become free from dirt; clean and pure.

Q. 54 : What are the misconceptions associated with meditation?

Sirshree : As soon as the word 'meditation' appears before us, many things associated with it appear in our mind, such as:

– Meditation means a hermit sitting with closed eyes in the Himalayas

– Meditation means sitting for hours at one place with eyes closed

– Meditation means difficult techniques

– Meditation means self-torture

– Meditation means something to be done after 50 years of age.

In this way, when a person hears some words or hears about something, then some ideas or conceptions form in his mind which perhaps he has heard, seen, read or thought about – many such things which he has accepted, but which are not true.

Everybody may have different misconceptions or everybody can have the same misconception. If you ask different people about meditation, perhaps everyone will give a different answer. All of the above points are misconceptions. There are many more.

Q. 55 : Can we attain wealth with meditation? Can we get a job or can we pass an examination due to meditation?

Sirshree : No, it's not that you will meditate and wealth will start pouring in or currency notes will start showering on you. Apparently there are some gurus who confound people with such misconceptions. There are such priests and pundits who have been teaching techniques of increasing money inflow in the name of spirituality. Because of such misconceptions, many people are pointlessly involved in such techniques and are wasting their time. Actually, meditation has got nothing to do with money. The capacity of earning money is different in every body-mind mechanism. Meditation may be helpful in enhancing your capacity and efficiency, but it does not happen that you will directly attain wealth or a job with meditation, nor will you directly get redemption for your sins with meditation.

Q. 56 : Why is it said that being 'here and now', in this very moment, is meditation?

Sirshree : Being 'here and now' is a preparation for meditation. That is why almost all techniques bring you to 'here and now.' If you watch your breath coming in and going out, then your mind will become focused and you will be able to remain in the present.

Q. 57 : But the mind does not stay focused on the breath; thoughts keep intruding.

Sirshree : That is why the mind is given something on which it will be able to focus, so that the number of thoughts can reduce. This will depend on practice. The more you practise, the more you can focus your mind. If your mind cannot stay focused on breathing, then you can give numbers to your breath.

For example: Give a number to every incoming breath. Take a breath and number it as '1.' Then you don't have to give a number to the outgoing breath. Then take another breath and number it as '2.' In this manner, when you are doing this for the first time, see if you are able to reach to the count of 50. Perhaps, you may lose your concentration in course. Then whenever you do it again, you will have a goal set for yourself to see what number you can reach this time. You will see that with practice, your count will go on increasing every time. Initially you should practise this technique with eyes closed. But later on, as you go on practising, you can do it even with your eyes open or while standing and even while walking.

Q. 58 : We feel bored with meditation.

Sirshree : If you feel bored, then what you have to understand is that this is also a trick of the mind. If you get fed up, then this too is a game of the mind and it is bound to happen. That is why until the mind gets habituated, the meditator should go wash his face, take a walk, and then sit to meditate again. You may have to do this until the mind develops a habit of meditation. Always be patient and keep a positive attitude. Don't worry about the result. You will definitely succeed.

PREPARATION FOR MEDITATION

Q. 59 : How many times in a day should we meditate and for how long?

Sirshree : It is good if you can meditate two times a day or at least once a day. If even once in a day is not possible, then at least three times a week.

The length of time for meditation should be at least 20 minutes, and for maximum benefit 45 minutes. For some special meditations, the period of time can be increased, especially for meditations that are done to improve concentration. As your practice grows with time, you can meditate for 45 minutes or even for an hour.

Q. 60 : Can the period of 20 minutes differ for different people?

Sirshree : Yes, if somebody's mind is very restless, then he may need to meditate for a longer period of time. For the average individual, a minimum of 20 minutes is appropriate to derive the right benefit of meditation. Anything less than that may not be enough. Otherwise it may so happen that you have sat down for meditation, and after some time you are fully prepared to go into the meditative state. But, it is time for you to get up. Then it's of no use. That is why at least 20 minutes have been recommended.

Q. 61 : Is it better if we meditate after taking a bath in the morning?

Sirshree : It helps when you try to bring sanctity in the process. If you see meditation as a sacred ritual and carry it out after having a bath, then it may prove very beneficial.

Q. 62 : It has been recommended to practise meditation sitting on a deerskin or a specific type of surface which is electricity resistant so that there is no loss of bodily electricity. How correct is this?

Sirshree : Some special types of meditations are practised for the purpose of enhancing physical powers or attaining occult powers. In such types of meditation, things like these become more important, where special attention is paid to the magnetic field of the body. The energy that is generated in the body of that person needs to be prevented from being pulled and sucked by the gravitational force of the Earth. Therefore something needs to be kept in between the body and the ground that can prevent the loss of that energy. In ancient times, yogis who used to practise meditation for long periods of time used to sit on a tiger skin or something similar. This was done so as to avoid wastage of the mental energy or the augmented physical energy that was generated through meditation.

Q. 63 : What factors need to be paid special attention to during meditation?

Sirshree : Initially during meditation, the factors that need to be paid special attention to are a fixed seat, place, time, posture, chanting of specific words, mantra, etc. Besides this, meditation should be practised daily and regularly. You should not keep changing your mantra or mudra every day. Whatever you have chosen (breathing, picture, mantra, repetition of a spiritual hymn, etc.) will help focus your mind and act as a support for you. If you have chosen one technique, then you should practise the same technique at the same time, same place, same seat, at least for a month. This will later prove very beneficial in meditation.

Q. 64 : Can I choose two techniques and practise one in the morning and the other in the evening?

Sirshree : Yes, you can do that. But even that should be fixed. It should not happen that one day you meditated in the morning and the other day in the evening. Also you should refrain from using the morning technique in the evening and the evening technique in the morning.

Q. 65 : You said that the technique we have chosen for the morning should be practised only in the morning and not in the evening. Why is that so?

Sirshree : Your mind does not pose any resistance in your daily routine activities such as rising from the bed in the morning, reaching for the wash basin, brushing your teeth, taking a bath, etc. This is because the mind has been made to develop the habit of all these activities. It has already been programmed for performing these tasks.

Similarly, the mind is being programmed for meditation. For example, when you go to a temple and join your hands together, then your whole body gets filled with the feelings of surrender. The whole body becomes helpful. If you inculcate the habit of continuity regarding meditation to the mind every day, then whenever you sit for meditation, the mind will get ready quickly without getting distracted. Due to a fixed time, seat, place and posture, the mind will become programmed and will then assist in the practice of meditation. Otherwise much time gets wasted in achieving steadiness of mind.

Q. 66 : The mind does not get focused quickly for meditation. What should be done for this?

Sirshree : For this, you should first find out which of your five senses is the most sensitive one, and then accordingly choose a meditation technique. There are different meditation techniques for each of the five senses. After having selected one, focus your mind on that sense. Due to this the mind will get interested and will thereby not distract you.

The reason for the discovery of different meditation techniques is that an appropriate meditation technique can be recommended to a person according to his most sensitive and most receptive sense organ. That is why there are different techniques for each sense. Like in some people, the sense of hearing, i.e. the ear is more sensitive and sharp. For them *japa* (repetition of spiritual syllables) will be more helpful. Some people's eyes are more sensitive, while others have a very sensitive and sharp nose. There are different meditations for each of them. In this way there are different meditation techniques for different senses.

Q. 67 : The sharper the senses, the better it is. Is that so?

Sirshree : Programming will be faster. And programming is the foundation. The more understanding you have, the better will be your programming and readiness. Senses are only a support for focusing the mind.

Q. 68 : Is meditation engaging the mind in something in which it is interested?

Sirshree : No, that is only a preparation for meditation. Initially, this is helpful in focusing the mind.

Q. 69 : Why has focusing on the breath been given so much importance in meditation?

Sirshree : The life energy that is present inside us is breath. It has been considered very important that we should be finely tuned with it because we are with it every moment. Our first task can be that we establish a tuning with that energy. Understanding the life energy and utilising it in life is possible only with a focused mind.

Breath is always available with us. We do not have a greed or desire for more breath; therefore breath is a 'pure' support. With the movement of breath in and out, we feel that we are alive. All these things add to the importance of breath. That is why focusing on the breath has been given more importance in various meditation techniques.

Q. 70 : After doing all this, how will I know that I have become focused?

Sirshree : Whenever you are performing any task, are you able to concentrate on it or do your thoughts take you onto some other topics? If your mind can stay focused for a long time on a given task, then your concentration is good. If you can concentrate even on things which the mind does not like, then your concentration is even better.

Q. 71: When will I know that I can now get off the concentration exercises and get on with meditation? When will I know whether I am ready for meditation?

Sirshree : If you begin the journey with concentration, then you will be taking steps one by one towards meditation. You are ready for meditation if: You are able to focus very easily for 20 minutes and also if you are able to increase the time period without any difficulty, if your mind gets focused as soon as you sit and even if thoughts arise they easily go away.

Q. 72 : When I sit to meditate for 20 minutes, I get a lot of thoughts. Then I feel I can't meditate properly. Can I meditate for 10 or 15 minutes?

Sirshree : A minimum of 20 minutes has been recommended because there will be at least some beginning of meditation in 20 minutes. You will at least be able to get a little closer to that experience. Duration of lesser than 20 minutes would not work. Suppose someone has come to deliver a discourse. All preparations are being made like setting up the stage, the microphone, etc. But when the preparations are complete, there is no time left for the discourse. Similarly, if we give less than 20 minutes for meditation, then we cannot benefit from it at all. The initial 10 minutes are spent in sitting and steadying the mind. The last 5 minutes are spent in getting ready to come out of meditation. So, if it is time for you to come out of meditation just when you are ready for it, you will not derive any benefit from it. Hence grant a minimum of 20 minutes so that you can get some advantage for at least 5 minutes.

MEDITATION AND INTELLECT

Q. 73 : What is the difference between meditation and contemplation? There is always a confusion associated with these words.

Sirshree : In English, the phrase "to meditate upon" has almost the same connotation as "contemplation". To meditate upon or to contemplate on signifies looking at a topic from all aspects or to go into the depth of a topic.

For instance, let us meditate upon a pen. This means to contemplate on the pen. How was the pen created? In ancient times, people used to write with sticks on the surface of leaves, but these were not very durable. Then they got the idea of ink. They began to write on paper with a wooden pen which had to be dipped in ink. But then the discovery was made to fill the ink in the pen rather than immersing the nib again and again in the ink. And the search is still going on. Many colours, shapes and sizes of pens are being created even today and it will continue even in the future... This is contemplation or meditating upon.

However, meditation is different from 'meditating upon' or contemplation. Contemplation (meditating upon) or concentration are tools to enter meditation. With the help of contemplation or a concentration technique such as looking at a pen or any other object for a long time, your mind becomes steady. Once your mind is steady and focused, you are then ready to enter the state of meditation or the state of nothingness.

Q. 74 : Then, is there no need for an intelligent person to meditate?

Sirshree : No, that is not so. When you begin to meditate, your concentration improves. An intelligent person may be able to easily contemplate, but less easily meditate. Contemplation is done by the mind. In meditation, the mind disappears. If you really have become focused, then you should get down to actual meditation.

Q. 75 : While meditating, I get a lot of ideas. Then I want to continue thinking about those ideas for some more time. Is this right?

Sirshree : No, this may become a hurdle for meditation. If it happens occasionally that you got an idea and took benefit from it, it is alright. But if it happens that you begin to meditate and always start pursuing ideas, then it is better that you set aside a separate time for idea generation.

Q. 76 : Can we see God by practising meditation?

Sirshree : This is a misconception. If you have your own ideas about the appearance of God, then you may certainly see Him in accordance with your imagination. During meditation, you may end up seeing God as per your idea of God because you may have thoughts such as, 'This is how God is. This is how his face is.' And if you are very attached to that face, then it is possible that you may see it. Mind can project this. A concentrated mind can do a lot of things for you. You will see a form; it may also speak to you. But actually, it is your mind that is speaking with you. The mind has found a support, which it is showing to itself. It has found a different medium. A Hindu will see Lord Rama, Krishna or Shiva and not Jesus. A Christian will see Jesus and not Rama. These are just projections of the mind... not experiencing God as it is.

Q. 77 : How will I know how much progress I have made in meditation?

Sirshree : When you talk about progress, then you are talking about meditation for concentration or increasing willpower and not real meditation. Your progress in this realm of meditation (concentration and willpower) can be seen by the following:

1. Your efficiency is increasing.
2. All your tasks are being completed faster because of complete awareness.
3. You are less absent-minded because you are more in the present.
4. Due to being single-minded and focused, your memory power is increasing; you can remember things, names, numbers and discourses better.
5. Also problem solving or decision making will be easier for you. Again this is because the mind is more focused.
6. If somebody asks you about how a particular thing should be done, then taking into consideration all the aspects associated with it, you will be able to take a good decision immediately.
7. You will feel a difference between your earlier life and your life now. You will feel that you are able to stay much happier now as compared to the past.
8. Self-control will increase and so will your patience.
9. You will feel more control over your body. Your body will be more disciplined. The intellect will become sharper and brighter. The mind will become purer.
10. You will be more serene in thoughts and during events.
11. You will start gaining victory over the defilements or corruptions of the mind.

After reading all of the above, if your interest has mounted and you want to know the depths of meditation in detail, then you can read the questions of seekers and the answers given to them regarding meditation in the chapters that follow.

As a child, everyone brings along the wealth of meditation, but due to ignorance of the importance of that wealth, we soon grow old. Meditation is becoming youthful in between these two states
where there is consciousness and awareness, where the understanding and importance of meditation is known.
Merciful is the one who has mercy.
Truthful is the one who has the truth.
Similarly, youthful is the one who has life, who is full of life.
Become youthful with meditation.

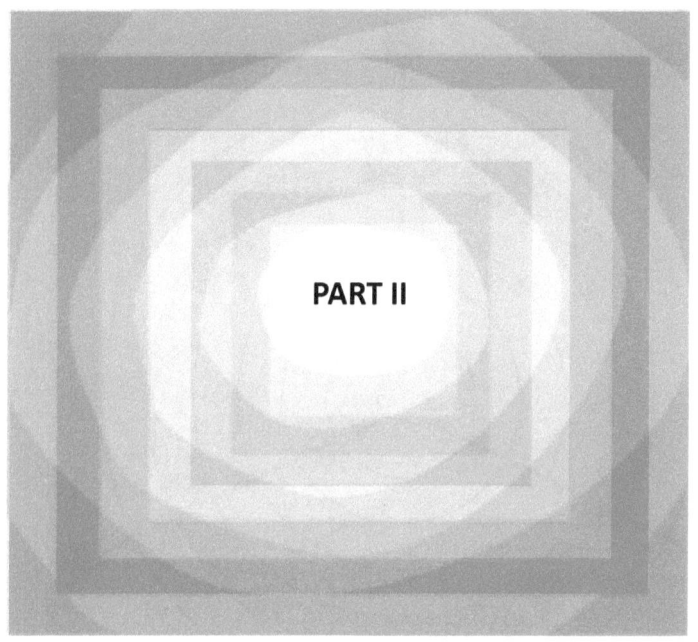

MEDITATION FOR SEEKERS

A seeker is one who is not only a lover of truth, but also wants to imbibe the truth in his life. Some questions that always trouble the seeker are: Who am I? Is this life restricted just to birth, actions, the fruits of those actions, and then death? Is all this a dream? What did it look like before this world came into existence? ...and many such questions.

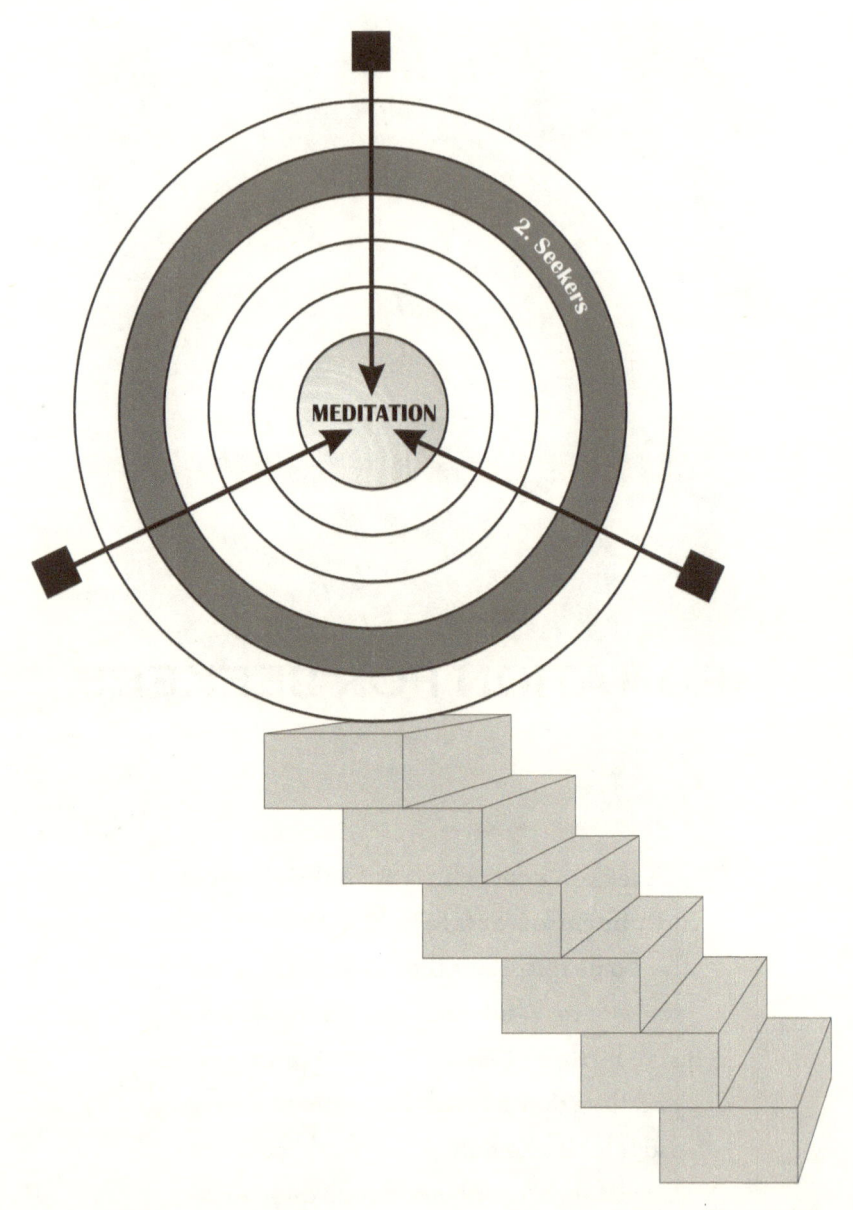

CHAPTER 9

From Meditation to Self Meditation

THE REAL GOAL

On what should a person meditate in life?
In life, there is nothing more worthy of meditation than 'life' – that life which is within you, within me, which is the 'being' of all.

Q. 78 : What is meditation?

Sirshree : Whenever we are entangled in the outside world – like in worldly objects, relations, wealth, status or power, then we are not in meditation. Meditation is a technique, a path that directs us from the outside world to within ourselves. When attention is directed outwards, then that is not meditation. But when attention is directed inwards, then that is meditation.

But when the eye sees outside, it gets identified with the external sights. When the ears listen outside, they get caught up with the external sounds. Similarly, the nose gets associated with the external scents. The tongue is eager for taste and the skin desires touch. All the senses are completely attracted to the outside world. Therefore there should be some technique that can liberate us from this outside world. But it is also important to understand that liberation from the outside world is not meditation. This is only preparation for meditation. That is why in most of the meditation techniques, it has been felt appropriate to practise meditation with eyes closed, or to sit in a soundproof room or in solitude or in a cave. All our senses should be redirected somehow from the outside world to return inside. But even that is just the initial preparation for entering meditation. Real meditation (Self Meditation) is that in which the eye returns onto the eye, i.e. the eye feels or experiences the eye; the ear should return onto the ear. All the senses should feel and experience themselves. When the senses are on themselves, they are then helpful for us to go within. We can then turn within very easily.

Q. 79 : What is real meditation (Self Meditation)?

Sirshree : Real meditation is the centre or source within oneself. Sometimes it is in the form of concentration and sometimes in the form of awareness. If we focus our meditation on external things, it is called attention. And if we turn our meditation within us, it is called awareness. Meditation means awakening that source. For example, just as exercise provides us with good health, in the same way:

– Meditation helps in keeping the mind balanced.

- Meditation helps in strengthening your faith and conviction.
- Meditation teaches you to come out of the past and future and stay in the present.
- Meditation increases your conviction that 'only the present is the truth'.

Q. 80 : How do we understand the depth of Self Meditation?

Sirshree : In order to understand the depth of Self Meditation, we will have to begin with external meditation. 'Self Meditation' is when meditation returns on meditation. When meditation is meditating on itself. When awareness is aware of itself. Meditation is a power. We begin to attract towards us whatever we turn the focus of meditation on. It does not matter if we meditate with awareness or without awareness. The thing that we are meditating upon is attracted towards us and starts proceeding towards us. But you cannot attain the Self Experience (existential experience or Experience of Being) with meditation, though meditation helps in enhancing the feeling of that experience.

Till today, many types of meditation techniques have been taught and recommended, seeing which many misconceptions about meditation have developed in our mind. Like when we hear a word 'Salvation (Moksh) Meditation,' we feel this is something very difficult, which is possible only after years of penance, which cannot be done by any ordinary person, which is not possible by a householder, we will have to leave everything aside and meditate for hours, we will have to renounce everything... All these are misconceptions. Many people want to see God during meditation. Although this is possible even through an optical illusion, but they want to do this in the name of spirituality. People firmly believe that this is what is meditation. In this way, one or the other misconception is associated with every meditation technique. The biggest misconception is that the 'meditation technique' is regarded as 'meditation' (Self Meditation).

(You can read in detail about Self Meditation in Part 4).

Q. 81 : If meditation techniques are not the real meditation (Self Meditation), then what is meditation?

Sirshree : Self Meditation is being one with the source or reaching the centre within. Techniques may be helpful in reaching that centre. And when you reach the centre, only then it can be said that 'you are in Self Meditation'. Only then is the meditation focused on meditation. Techniques will be helpful only to the extent of your level of understanding. Many such techniques have been discovered which make reaching the centre simple and easy as well as help you in raising your level of understanding.

DISCOVERY OF MEDITATION

Q. 82 : When did the search for meditation begin?

Sirshree : Till today, many generations have lived on this Earth and it has been observed that every man is in search of something. His search began since he was living in the jungles. Then he began changing himself – into a man who is searching all the time for happiness, for achieving something… every moment a new joy that will make him better. This search has progressed and has evolved today in the form of an advanced man. His search is for making today better than yesterday and tomorrow better than today. He adopted 'meditation' as part of this search. Meditation is a method which can give a person such information about his present or his past that will make his tomorrow better.

Q. 83 : For what kind of people is the path of meditation?

Sirshree : The path of meditation is for those people who are willing to wait today in order to try to make a better tomorrow. Meditation is such a path which, if traversed in the right manner, can lead a person to his ultimate goal.

Before solving any problem, it is essential to understand the problem fully. Likewise, before living life it is essential to understand it completely. This is the role of meditation. Meditation is a path to understand life completely. To meditate means to create a new life for ourselves, which will reveal to us the secret of the art of life. One may get fifty problems in his life which he may solve grudgingly. Though the problems may be solved, one may still not be successful. However, out of fifty problems if we solve even five problems in the right manner, then we are successful. A problem is like a guest who can drop in at any time. What is important is that we should achieve mastery in solving problems. Meditation is for those who want to achieve this mastery.

Q. 84 : What is the 'real mastery' or art of solving problems?

Sirshree : Before solving a problem, it is important to know the art of solving problems. That means now we are ready for any problem. If we have learnt this art, it means we are successful. For example, a student appears for examinations many times in his life and every time he prepares for his exams with dread in his mind. He gets good grades in his exams, but still he won't be considered as successful since his fear remains. On the contrary, even if he gets fewer marks but gets rid of his fear of exams, then he is a successful person. This is 'real mastery'. Because more important than passing or failing in examinations is the development of self-confidence, which gives you the courage to face any problem.

The fact is that problems will keep cropping up in life. The question is, how do you solve them – grudgingly or gladly? Meditation gives us that perspective, that courage, that self-confidence, which will liberate us from those fears. We become ready to live life in a new way.

Q. 85 : Can we know our inner secrets with meditation?

Sirshree : Yes, meditation can help us know such things about ourselves, which other people are either unable to know about themselves or it is not easy for them to know. Meditation enhances our awareness; due to which our awareness increases for everything. We find ourselves more at peace and more stable.

Meditation brings a change in our thoughts. The chaos that exists in thoughts reduces to a great extent. A simplicity seeps in. Thinking power intensifies. Many things about the mind become clear to us, which otherwise we would have never known. But a bigger secret is 'Who am I?' and meditation helps in finding the answer to this question.

Q. 86 : What is reality?

Sirshree : Reality is being (existence). It means to abandon 'becoming" and get into a state of just being.

Q. 87 : What will we achieve after doing all this?

Sirshree : You will get 'nothing' because the meaning of meditation is 'doing nothing'. Till today, you have never bought 'nothing'. Do at least something in life for which you will get nothing. The mind has always done only those things through which it can achieve something. By doing meditation, for the first time you do something for which you will get nothing. That means you sow the seed of something new, which will bear a different fruit. But you don't have to do this out of expectation for the fruit. Yes, you shall definitely get physical and mental benefits like freedom from stress, greater concentration power and higher efficiency. This will improve your business. Improved business means more money. Concentration power increases, due to which memory power increases, and the unsteadiness of mind decreases. When you practise meditation, you will gradually be able to see all these benefits in your life. You will find that earlier you used to forget some things, but now, you don't. An awareness comes in. But our focus should not be on the benefits, but on experiencing the taste of nothing.

Q. 88 : What is the difference between meditation and concentration?

Sirshree : Concentration is the path for preparation of meditation, for going towards meditation. Meditation is the destination. We have to get stabilised on the Self; we have to get the experience of being. If the mind is concentrated, then it will be supportive in attaining meditation. That means even our body-mind mechanism will cooperate in attaining the experience.

Q. 89 : From where did meditation originate? We have heard that Lord Shiva told all the meditation techniques to Parvati and 'Vigyan Bhairav Tantra' has emerged from that. Who was the first guru who told it is essential to practise meditation?

Sirshree : Meditation has come down from the sages. Meditation began in the era of the sages or when man began to know the truth. Shiva and Parvati are just the indications or symbols of the truth.

Q. 90 : Since sages have been mentioned here, a question arises as to what is the difference between meditation and *japa* (silent repetition of mantras or spiritual syllables)?

Sirshree : In *japa*, a word is taken and repeated. Meditation is a technique without words. Actually, *japa* is the act of Being which should take us towards *ajapa* (constant spontaneous remembrance of the Self without words), because that is the essence, which has to be realised.

MEDITATION – EGO – KUNDALINI

Q. 91 : Sirshree, I am worried about something. I have some relatives and acquaintances who meditate for even ten days at a stretch. But there has been no change in their behaviour. Instead, they have become more egoistic. My question is what detriments can occur with meditation? What are its disadvantages?

Sirshree : There is an intrinsic danger associated with meditation techniques if there is no understanding associated with them. That is why instead of being beneficial, they can be harmful. Because the person who is doing meditation may feel that:

— I am the one who meditates

- I am the meditator
- I am superior to others
- Those who are not practising meditation are inferior

Thus he may feel superior and want to improve others. He will go around telling people, "You are not meditating! You should practise meditation."

Due to this, you may feel that there has been no change in these people who are practising meditation. Instead meditation has become more dangerous for them. When *siddhis* (occult powers) appear in a person through meditation, then meditation will be very misleading for him and become the cause of his downfall. His main aim is left aside. Now that his mind has achieved some powers, he would like to develop those powers and thus gets entangled in them. He would completely miss the reality.

The one who gets entangled in *siddhis* thinks, "Now I can read people's minds. By looking at their faces I can tell what is going on in their minds." Then he will meet various people and tell them, "You are thinking so and so." People will be impressed with him and he will get obsessed with false ego. If he gets stuck with developing these mystical powers, then his real aim will be left behind and forgotten. This is the second great danger.

Q. 92 : Then there is another question in relation to these risks that we have heard that *kundalini* gets activated with meditation. Is the activation of the *kundalini* right or wrong?

Sirshree : Real meditation has no relation whatsoever with *kundalini*. This is because the Reality or Truth is a phenomenon beyond the body-mind mechanism. 'Being' has nothing to do with the body or mind. Body-mind mechanism is a great wonder in itself. If man starts working on it, then his whole life will be spent on it. He won't be left with any time to know the reality because the body-mind has so many secrets, so many powers. A concentrated mind in itself is a miracle; it can perform many a great feat.

Q. 93 : Then why have so many of its negative aspects been highlighted, emphasising not to activate the *kundalini* and so on?

Sirshree : The goal is to 'know oneself, recognise the Self'. If somebody forgets the goal and gets engrossed in arousing powers, then the individual (the one who feels apparent separateness from the rest of the creation) becomes egoistic and strong. Actually, the individual has to efface and melt away. The individual ego has to be transcended. But, in this case, with the awakening of powers, the individual becomes even more strong. He will indulge in just fulfilling his desires. You are not able to fulfil your desires because you don't have the required resources. That is why you are sitting quiet. But if such a power awakens in you (i.e. if you get Aladdin's magic lamp), then you won't be able to sit quiet. You would definitely want to fulfil all your desires as soon as possible and then you would be totally absorbed in that.

Q. 94 : Sirshree, I don't know if it is favourable or detrimental, but I have also heard that by practising meditation, some people get 'out of body experiences' or sometimes they even begin to fly? Is this true?

Sirshree : This is called astral projection. If you are practising meditation with the aim of astral traveling, then that is not the aim of true meditation. Its goal has become different. That means you are trying to arouse the powers of your mind. You are not meditating for the sake of meditation. Where there is a desire to attain something, an aspiration to achieve something, then that is not meditation; because there is no desire to achieve anything in meditation.

Q. 95 : Even when we meditate without any desire to achieve anything, sometimes we are able to see a light and we feel as if God has appeared!

Sirshree : Then at that time you have to ignore it. You don't have to show any interest in it. If you continue having interest in it, then you will get involved in developing it and subsequently miss the real thing. Just ask yourself, "Who is the one who sees the light?"

Q. 96 : What is the difference between Samadhi and meditation?

Sirshree : If you consider meditation from the perspective that it is 'to be done', then meditation is a path and Samadhi is the destination. But if you consider the real meaning of meditation, then 'meditation' is an attribute of the original state of our being (Samadhi). Water is wet, then what relation do you associate between 'wetness' and 'water'? Water is transparent, then how do you relate these two entities? Likewise, the relation between 'meditation' and 'your being' or 'Consciousness' which is within you is that 'meditation' is an intrinsic quality or an attribute of 'Consciousness'.

When 'meditation' returns on 'meditation,' which means when Consciousness returns on itself, then taking this meaning into consideration, the word 'meditation' was coined. In the beginning, an individual does not know anything about himself, therefore he is told that you have to 'practise meditation' to reach somewhere, to know something. In this way, the path and the destination are taken as two different entities. Actually, when we say that water is transparent, then we can't take 'transparent' as a path nor 'water' as the destination. Hence 'practise meditation' means know your own attribute.

MEDITATION AND MISCONCEPTIONS

Q. 97 : Can I attain Self Realisation with meditation?

Sirshree : Yes, with meditation you will reach that point where there will appear a state of Samadhi. Gradually, you will develop conviction in it, and if reverence arises within you then it becomes all the more easier to go onto oneself. In the end, you will know that 'meditation is your nature, which was present since the very beginning.'

Q. 98 : I am not able to do Vipassana Meditation these days. What should I do? And because I am unable to meditate, I have developed a feeling of guilt.

Sirshree : Who is meditating, know that first.

Q. 99 : I used to meditate!

Sirshree : First know who is this 'I', then you will forever remain in meditation. Or rather you will become meditation. You will become devotion itself.

Q. 100 : I did not understand this.

Sirshree : That's okay. You will have to listen from the beginning. You will have to listen, keeping all your false beliefs aside and without making comparisons. Then you will understand that meditation of the Witness is constantly going on. There is awareness of unawareness and also awareness of awareness – Bright awareness beyond both. Bright awareness is meditation. You don't have to do meditation, just understand that you are meditation.

Q. 101 : We won't have to do meditation?

Sirshree : Not just meditation, you will get freedom from every type of deed (*karma*). You will get the understanding that you were never the doer, then how will you be the doer of meditation?

Q. 102 : What should we do to get this understanding?

Sirshree : You will have to go through the whole process of this 'understanding' in which you will have to learn the First Foundation Truth. After that you can attend the 'Maha Aasmani Retreat'. All the things will be told step by step and you will have to contemplate on each of them. Guidance is essential; because without guidance many people are stuck with just the techniques for a prolonged length of time. Without guidance a long period of time is required.

Everyone's Gita* is different. When you listen to your own Gita, i.e. what is useful only for you, then it will happen very fast. Like you asked the question if meditation is the best method. The answer is that if your Gita includes that your mind is very unsteady, easily distractible, can't focus on anything – then from that viewpoint you are told that meditation may be the best and the fastest method; but not for others; it may be misleading for others.

— Everyone's Gita is different because everyone's physical and mental constitution is different. Some people can sleep well after taking a bath at night while others feel refreshed after a bath and cannot sleep because the nature of every body has been created differently. The Gita which is right for Arjuna, is not right for Duryodhana or Shakuni.

— Everyone's Gita is also different because everybody's beliefs and misconceptions are different. For instance, some people believe in form, some in formless, some in destiny and some in deeds (*karma*). Some people believe that selfless service is most important, while others feel that chanting the Lord's name is everything. Some people feel that talismans or ashes is spirituality, while others believe that singing hymns and holy songs is devotion to God. That is why everyone's Gita is different. (For example, in the Mahabharata if instead of Arjuna, Duryodhana would have come to Lord Krishna, then would Lord Krishna have said exactly the same things that He told Arjuna? No, the Gita would have changed in that case).

---

*Gita: The holy text which contains guidance provided by Lord Krishna to Arjuna. Here it implies the body-mind makeup, the tendencies, the understanding level, the state of each individual is different, hence the guidance appropriate for each is different.

Q. 103 : I can undertake a self-development course for improving my concentration. Then why should I practise meditation?

Sirshree : A self-development course will certainly be useful for improving your concentration. But it won't help you know the answer to 'Who am I?' Your concentration power will rise, but your senses will not get habituated to turn within. You did a self-development course and it helped you strengthen your willpower. How will that affect you? You will be able to complete all your tasks in a better way. Your control over your body will increase. 'I have to go within myself or I want to know myself" – this is not the aim for which you are doing a self-development course; these things are not within its domain. But with meditation, your intention right from the beginning is: I want to go within and I want to know 'Who am I?' That is why I need to concentrate my mind, so that I develop the habit of going within.

Q. 104 : But people have told me to practise meditation for upgrading my concentration and memory.

Sirshree : If a new person is told to practise meditation, then what kind of motivation does he need? What inspiration should be given to him? For instance, if you want to convince a child for meditation, then you will have to tell him that he will get a toy in return. If it's a student, you will have to tell him that his future will be bright with meditation. That will be inspiring for him. You will tell a sick person that he will become healthy again. At least, people will make a beginning with this kind of motivation. When he will come to know that he can accomplish even the 'final goal of life' with meditation, he will feel, why not go for it? Let us understand this with the example of a television:

A television set is kept in a room, but people don't know anything about televisions. Hence it is just lying around in a corner. Then one day somebody switches it on and increases its volume. He is amazed,

'Wow! It plays songs,' and he is very pleased. Since there is one more option in the television, he enhances the brightness control, which makes him realise that the television also has a screen, due to which now there is some light in the room. If you inform him that it also has the possibility of displaying pictures, and you attach it with an antenna, then black and white pictures appear, and he becomes very happy. You further tell him that it has even more possibilities such as it can show colours, and then colours appear. He is absolutely delighted. Then you tell him it has many different channels; also it can display screen on screen due to which he can watch two channels at the same time… In this way, you tell him everything one by one.

Q. 105 : Is it essential to have a Guru, a spiritual master, for meditation?

Sirshree : Actually, a Guru is needed in every path, no matter which path is being followed. The books that you read at school, the same books you can also sit at home and read, but how much time will that take? Supposing, a child decides he will not go to school at all, he will study up to the tenth grade at home. Then what do you feel, in how many years will he be able to complete his tenth grade? Everything is written in books. The teachers in the school are also going to teach what is in the syllabus. The entire syllabus is available in the books. Questions are going to be asked in the examination from this syllabus alone. But then the child finds that he has more difficulties when he does not go to school.

In the path of meditation, everything is within the mind, and its syllabus is not even written anywhere. Additionally, everyone's syllabus is different. That is why here it becomes even more essential to have a Guru, a teacher.

MEDITATION AND MUDRAS

Q. 106 : Many *mudras* (symbolic hand gestures) have been discovered for meditation. Were all these mudras meant for attaining *siddhis* (occult powers) alone?

Sirshree : No, not just for *siddhis*. But *mudras* have many other benefits too. It becomes a habit for the body that if you sit in a particular *mudra*, then a particular state will manifest. If you sit in *gyan mudra* (wisdom posture), then the physical change will act as an indication and bring about the desired effect.

For instance, if a student studies at the same place and in the same posture every day, then gradually he will start feeling that his concentration is improving. Similarly, if somebody is able to associate a particular state of mind with the *mudra* of joining the thumb and index finger, then he will be able to generate that state whenever he wishes to. The next time, he only has to join his thumb and index finger. If somebody associates the state of self-confidence with the *mudra*, then he will be able to feel self-confidence anywhere... on the stage, in an interview, while driving, and so on.

Q. 107 : Does this mean that by adopting a particular mudra, we can make our journey towards the ultimate goal?

Sirshree : Yes. Supposing you always practise meditation using a particular mudra. Then with the help of that particular mudra, you can recall the meditative state as many times as you wish in a day. Even in routine life, if you just want to relax, then too you can use that mudra. If you switch to that mudra, then the body goes into relaxation. The mind can also become calm. If suddenly a crisis arises, then you can switch to the mudra to go into a relaxed state, even if you are not sitting or closing your eyes. The mudra will act as a 'relax button', as a relaxation trigger.

MEDITATION AND MISERY

Q. 108 : Do our mental miseries end with the practice of meditation?

Sirshree : Mental misery means false beliefs and misconceptions. With meditation, if the understanding grows of 'Who am I?' then it is freedom from all misconceptions. With freedom from all misconceptions, all miseries and mental troubles come to an end.

Q. 109 : How far can meditation help in physical problems?

Sirshree : We have physical problems and sufferings because of our identification with our body. We believe ourselves to be this body. That is why we have physical pains and sufferings. The moment our identification with our body breaks, physical sufferings will cease to exist.

The body is the image of the true Self. A sick body also works as a mirror for us just like a healthy body. If we have this understanding, then the physical sufferings will markedly reduce, which otherwise used to get multiplied several times due to our identification with the body. There are pains and these pains will remain. But due to our identification with the body we get the feeling, 'I have pain,' and thus the pain becomes a suffering. It is only when the word 'I' gets associated, do we feel all these sufferings and miseries. One aspect is "there is pain" and the other is "I have pain". There is a lot of difference between the two.

Q. 110 : This means that we can even get rid of sufferings of old age and miseries of hospitalisations with meditation?

Sirshree : Yes, you can certainly get rid of these, but you can even be liberated from death.

When we married our body, then all the new relationships came into existence. Here 'married' implies that we accepted the body as 'I,' due to which all the in-laws standing behind it appeared in our life –

i.e. the physical sufferings and mental miseries. If we don't establish a relation with 'I', then no relation exists with all of these.

MISTAKES IN MEDITATION

Q. 111 : What kind of mistakes are usually committed by people who practise meditation?

Sirshree : The biggest mistake in the practice of meditation has been whereupon the individual ego becomes stronger. So the ultimate aim is not at all accomplished. The purpose for which you had embarked on the journey, that itself was not achieved. Everything else was achieved. This is the biggest blunder that can occur in the path of meditation. Why is that so? The reason is awakening of powers. A concentrated mind is a great power. It can accomplish many feats. If a man can do anything, he can do it only with a concentrated mind. All the powers which you must have heard such as *reiki*, occult powers (*siddhis*), healing powers, etc. are the result of a concentrated mind. A concentrated mind can arouse many powers. Although there are many benefits of these powers, the journey was not begun to attain all these benefits. Hence it is said that this is a major loss. Let us understand this with the help of an example. If you went to the beauty parlour for Self Realisation and came back only feeling fresh, that means the purpose for which you went there was not met. That is why it has been emphasised that it should not happen that you start liking the benefits so much that they become your goal. By indulging in them, you get so influenced by them that you start saying, "I want this... I want more... and more."

Q. 112 : Many people try to maintain awareness in whatever they are doing the whole day. So far, you haven't said anything about that. Is it that these people are not clear about their aim? Is this also a mistake?

Sirshree : The real aim is to know oneself. The awareness of the concentrated mind increases, which means you become aware about 'What am I doing?' So when getting up, you say, 'I am getting up.'

When sitting, you are aware that 'I am sitting.' When talking, 'I am talking.' When lying down, 'I am lying down,' and so forth. It is natural for the concentrated mind to be aware in such things. But if someone is making this awareness of his activities as his goal, then he is making a mistake. In many types of spiritual practices, it has been said that whatever you are doing, do it with awareness. Be aware while taking a bath, while walking be aware of the touch of the ground, feel the air, feel what is happening. If one is able to do this, then he feels very happy thinking that 'something is happening with me' or 'I am achieving something.' But he is under a great illusion because the practice of being aware of all these things was with the intention of being aware of oneself. He should be able to be 'aware for the Self'; being aware for awareness, being full of awareness, being filled with a feeling of 'Self Witness' – this was the primary goal.

Q. 113 : What is the meaning of 'Witness'?

Sirshree : 'Witness' is the most basic word for meditation. Reference to this word exists in every spiritual book. To have the feeling of a Witness means using something external as a channel to return to the Self. 'Self-Witness' is then a more appropriate word. Now the word 'Witness' has lost its true significance. Whoever created this word did not know that it will become corrupted in this manner, and hence 'Self-Witness' is an appropriate word for it today.

Returning onto the Self-Witness means using external things as a means to get stabilised on the Self. Just as external sights indicate towards the eye; they remind us that we have eyes. Sound makes us aware that we have ears. But without getting involved in sounds, return to the ears. Without getting involved with the sights, return to the eyes. Without getting involved with smell, return to the nose. Without getting involved with taste, return to the tongue. Without getting engrossed in thoughts, we have to know the one who is watching the thoughts, the one who is aware of thoughts, the one who is eternally awake, the one who is knowing. No senses are present there. It cannot be known with eyes or the ears. External sight is an indication or pointer to return onto that ultimate source. But because of ignorance, because of lack of understanding, the indication that we are constantly getting is not received by us. It appears as if that indication is not coming to us. This is the illusion that gets created.

Q. 114 : Meditation or the technique of meditation has been associated with the 'third eye' or *aagya chakra*, so what is its role and what is its objective?

Sirshree : When the *chakras* (energy vortices) of the body are activated from the *muladhara* up to the *sahasra chakra*, then the 'third eye' (*aagya chakra*) is also important in the process. It has been beneficial. But these techniques are associated with the body. As stated earlier, the body is also a wonder in itself. All these *chakras* (seven *chakras*) are related to the body. The mind is made to concentrate on these *chakras* so that the energy within them is activated. Actually, every *chakra* with its special power has its importance. But for 'real meditation' all these things are not required.

THE REAL GOAL

Q. 115 : Sirshree, can we give the real meditation a unique name that is different from all other meditation techniques and also signifies our ultimate aim?

Sirshree : The new word can be *Swa-dhyan*, which means Self Meditation or meditation on Self. It is just like the word Self-Witness has been coined which gives the right description of the Witness. Likewise, real meditation can be called Self Meditation or Tej Meditation. The word 'meditation' is retained and not changed because people are already familiar with this word. When you ask a person whether he does meditation or Self Meditation, he will think and ponder over it and say, "Yes! I do Self Meditation, which means meditation on the Self."

Q. 116 : What is the real goal of man? What are the obstacles in achieving it? And what are the things that help us in reaching the goal?

Sirshree : The real goal is to know 'Who am I?'

– To know that which is beyond the body, mind and intellect
– To know that which is our Being, our Consciousness, the 'Real I'
– To know that which is the unlimited
– To know that which is beyond personal ego
– To know that which is the 'Universal I' – where there is the feeling of oneness

To get stabilised in that state is the actual aim, the real goal of man. Keeping that goal in mind, all these meditation techniques were discovered. Meditation becomes automatic when you have reached the goal. Actually, meditation is the fruit, the result after reaching the ultimate goal of Self Realisation and Self Stabilisation. This is because meditation is an intrinsic quality of the Self. Once Self Realisation and Self Stabilisation is attained, you are always in meditation; or rather you become meditation. When there is direct talk with the truth seekers, they are told, 'Meditation is the destination and not the path.' This means meditation is the end in itself, not a means to an end.

But it has been adopted as a path and the discussion is, what kind of a path is it? If in the beginning we are considering it as a path, then it will continue to be regarded and understood as a path.

The goal of human life is opening, blossoming, and playing, i.e. to explore all the possibilities within you, which is possible through meditation. The complete possibility of man is – he will fully open up, fully blossom up and play. This means that he will realise that God's game is going on upon this Earth and he is a part of that game. After realisation, he now begins to play the game with the understanding of the truth, then the whole-sole purpose of man will be achieved. Every being on Earth has begun on this path. Every flower in the garden is blossoming. It is another thing that before blossoming fully, some flowers get broken from the stem, some are blown away by the winds, some get plucked by kids, and some are eaten away by worms. But the goal of each flower is to blossom fully and spread its essence with the help of winds to one and all.

To blossom completely in life, to achieve this goal, we should look around to see what system, what arrangement is present which we can utilise to reach our goal as fast as possible. This is the goal of human life, the goal of each and every one of us. Because this is not clear to us, we don't work on this. If this becomes clear, then our 'meditation' will begin. We then won't lose a single opportunity that will help in our progress. We won't miss a single discourse that will take us further towards our goal. Listening to spiritual discourses, service, devotion, prayer, meditation will become very easy for us.

This may be the question of everyone since everyone has to fully open up and blossom. Whatever one can do, one should do. You should not think about what others can do. A daisy does not think about a rose. What you actually are and what that real you can do – this is what you should think about.

There are five obstacles that prevent us from reaching our goal:

1. Ignorance
2. Unawareness
3. Bad company
4. Wrong actions and mistakes committed in this life
5. Tendencies. Tendencies means such patterns or habits that are deeply rooted in our body-mind, due to which we keep on repeating the same things without awareness. For example,

somebody swears at us, we swear back in return, because that has been programmed in our mind, we are not even aware of it. It has become a tendency.

There are five things that are helpful in achieving our goal:

1. Self-Enquiry. If you constantly practise Self-Enquiry, you will understand the difference between real and unreal. Ask yourself, "Who am I? Who felt bad? Who felt good? Whatever happened, happened with whom?"
2. Contemplation
3. Awakening our power of discrimination (*viveka*)
4. Group or team. Group means such a team in which all are walking the path of truth with the same objective in mind and where the level of consciousness is high. Such a group will take us towards our ultimate goal.
5. Spiritual discourses, where the truth is being spoken of, where you come to know who you really are. The Real Discourses, the Final Discourses help you in this.

GOAL OF MEDITATION

Every person wants happiness, that is why he tries to find a reason to be happy.

His happiness is in :

– getting appreciated
– celebrating festivals and parties
– winning the bumper prize of a lottery
– getting cured from a disease
– someone accepting what he says
– getting a promotion at work
– things happening according to his wishes

- an obstacle getting removed from his path
- listening to and telling a hilarious joke
- hurting an enemy
- going to parks, picnics, movies
- eating a variety of delicacies in restaurants and hotels
- shopping for items of the latest fashion
- being fashionable and wearing new dresses
- receiving and decorating awards on the shelf
- celebrating birthdays and receiving gifts
- receiving jewels and jewelry
- giving birth to children
- reconciling with an upset friend

But there is real happiness that is without any reason.
- It is not because of losing something nor because of gaining something
- It is the happiness that does not diminish with time
- It is the happiness that goes on increasing with time
- The happiness because of a reason disappears as soon as the reason disappears; it will leave sorrow in its wake
- But how can the happiness without reason disappear?
- It won't go anywhere nor will it bring any sorrow
- To attain this happiness is the goal of man
- This is the real treasure of meditation attained due to Self Meditation.

One should meditate by oneself
Or is is that 'being oneself' is meditation?
Being on oneself is where duality ends.
When duality ends, then who is there to be
called as 'one?' Then even the 'one' ends.
This then is 'being oneself' where even the 'one'
ends.

CHAPTER 10

Witness Self-Witness

LANGUAGE AND WORDS

Wealth is a path, not the destination.
Meditation is the destination, not a path.
Wealth is everything, yet nothing.
Meditation is nothing, yet everything.

Q. 117 : Explain in detail about Witness, Self-Witness?

Sirshree : A boy showed a bulb to his friend and asked him, "Can you light this bulb without electricity, without battery, and without a wire?" The friend answered, "Definitely not; this is impossible. Can you light it?"

The boy replied, "Yes, this is possible. Just put it into the fire and it will light up."

In this example, the friend took the meaning of the word 'lighting' in the light of his old knowledge. Therefore, the Guru has to break the old words.

Knowing the mind and knowing about the mind are two different types of knowledge. If you want to know *about* the mind, then only the mind can know about the mind, but if you want to know the mind, then you will have to detach from the mind (and be what you are) to examine the mind. You don't have to take help from the mind for this purpose. You have to take help from a Bright Perceptor (*Tej Parkhi**). When you are looking at the world, then the world becomes an object and the eye is the 'see-er.' But the mind is knowing through the eyes, then the eye becomes the object and the mind becomes the 'knower'. But when the mind itself becomes the object, then awakens the Self-Witness (Bright Witness). Self-Witness is knowing the mind, but its purpose is not knowing the mind or its world. Its purpose is to know its own self. If the 'tongue' is told to taste itself, then what would it do? It cannot do this. But

---

*Tej Parkhi – the one who has the eye to see the Final Truth. The vision to understand the truth as it is and differentiate between the truth and untruth. The sight to go beyond true and false and experience the Bright Truth. Only a goldsmith has the eye that differentiates between fake and real jewelry. The one who possesses such an eye, such vision, such perception, such sight is called as "*parkhi*". This vision is not connected to 'seeing' but to 'deep knowing'. The one who possesses such a vision and who is beyond knowledge and ignorance is called *Tej Parkhi* or Bright Perceptor.

the Self-Witness (Self) can do this. It does this by using the body-mind as a medium or an instrument. Just like the eye for seeing the eye uses a mirror as a medium or an instrument.

Because of not having this insight, people try to know the mind through the mind and become unsuccessful. Due to not knowing these aspects, many hypocrite gurus, by providing the wrong meaning of 'witnessing', misguide the disciples. They do not explain the meaning of 'Witness' as 'Self-Witness' and ask the disciples to be a Witness to see external things. In this way, by focusing on things external, the disciple remains entangled in them all his life. The true guru is the Self-Witness itself and he makes his disciple also a Self-Witness. He makes the disciple know that what he is searching for is 'he himself' (the Self).

Q. 118 : Why does the Guru change the words?

Sirshree : When the Guru changes the old vocabulary, then some seekers become suspicious as to why the words of the old scriptures are being changed. They feel this is wrong. Such doubts are a hurdle in the disciple's path.

In this case, the Guru's answer is that when something is told to you in old words, then you also listen to it with your old understanding. You have already constructed and fixed the meaning of every word in your mind. You have already defined every word. Therefore, when somebody utters words like 'soul,' 'Witness,' 'knowledge,' 'destiny,' 'Guru,' 'love,' 'God' or 'meditation,' then you take only the old meaning of these words, which brings no change in your ignorance. A real guru snatches away not only your ignorance, but also your knowledge, and takes you beyond both.

The mind becomes the boss
when Consciousness goes to sleep.
The mind becomes a servant
when Consciousness, backed by the strength of
meditation, announces itself as the boss.

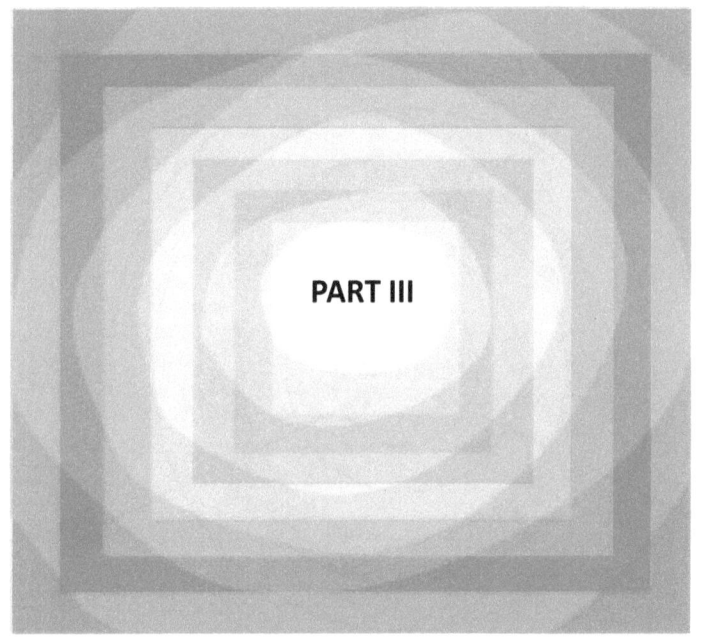

PART III

MEDITATION FOR DISCIPLES

When the understanding of a seeker gets
deeper, then his journey begins towards the
truth in the form of a disciple. A disciple
is one who always lives in his head, who
is understanding meditation through his
intellect. His understanding has not yet come
down at the experiential level.
Yet he follows the path he has chosen.

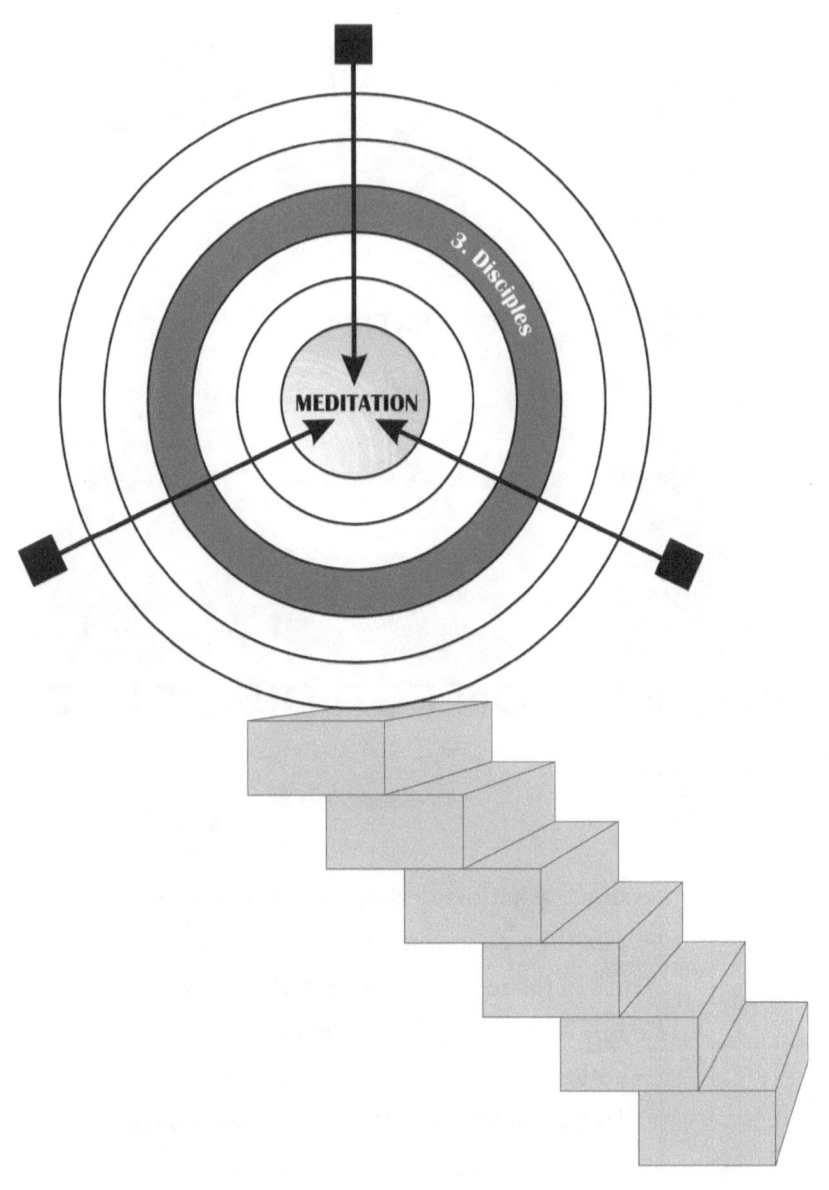

CHAPTER 11
First Truth
SENSE OF BEING

Nobody knows what death is and that is why people are afraid of dying. We do not know what happens in meditation, that is why our mind is scared of jumping into it. After attaining understanding, it becomes easy for the mind to enter the unknown. Therefore, before going into the depths of meditation, attain the understanding of the truth. Listen to the truth, take refuge at the feet of a living guru. Only then can you travel into the unknown, without hesitation or fear.

> **Note:**
> What you are going to read from hereon, may possibly change your life. You may discover the purpose for which you were born. That is how important the 'First Truth' is. While reading this book, read everything that is written, be it a punctuation mark or a space between two words. In fact, try to grasp even that which is not visible.

Q. 119 : Who am I?

Sirshree : If this question is asked from you, then one of the answers that appears is: "I am this body." When we look into the mirror, we see our body and we feel, 'This is me.' Let us understand this through an example and contemplate on it.

- If a person loses both his arms and legs, then is he there? Is he complete or incomplete?

- If he loses his eyes, his hearing, his tongue, is he still there? Is he still complete from within?

- If his kidney has been removed by surgery, if he has got an artificial heart transplant, does he still feel complete? Think over it.

Q. 120 : Does this mean that I am not this body?

Sirshree : We have heard earlier that 'I am not this body' but is this seen in our conduct? Or are we saying it just for the sake of saying that "I am not this body." If you have really believed it, then even your behavior would have been accordingly. That is why, today, we will clarify the first question, "Am I this body or am I something else?"

The only thing that really exists is 'I am' or beingness. But man has the misunderstanding that he is the body-mind, and till the end of his life, he does not know that whom he believed to be 'I' was not actually I. Just imagine that if one day you find out that what you believed yourself to be, is actually not you, then how would you feel at that time? That means all your life you were thinking 'This is I' and then you came to know that it is not so, then what will happen? What a havoc it would create inside you! Will something happen or not? You had believed in this for so many years. Man begins with his body and asks, "Am I this body?," then how will it be decided that 'I am not this body'? Let us take a simple example for this... There is a pencil in my hand, can you see this pencil?

Q. 121 : Yes, I can see it. So?

Sirshree : Are you this pencil?

Q. 122 : How can I be this pencil?!

Sirshree : Why do you say that you are not this pencil?

Q. 123 : Because my soul is not in this pencil.

Sirshree : Can you see the soul? Do you know the soul?

Q. 124 : No... no.

Sirshree : Then how did you say that my soul is not in it? Now tell me why you cannot be this pencil.

Q. 125 : The pencil is outside my body.

Sirshree : This means what is outside the body is 'not I', conversely what is inside the body is 'I'. Okay, this is an answer. But can there also be another answer such as this pencil is an object and the observer is somebody else, which means the observer can never be the object. Are you understanding this point? You can see the pencil, which means you are not the pencil. So, can you see the body?

Q. 126 : Yes, everybody can see the body, so what?

Sirshree : You can see the body, the body is visible, does that mean you are this body? If you were the body, then how would you be able to see the body? The subject sees the object. (Only a seer (see-er) can see the object). Think! Think!! Then who is seeing?

Q. 127 : The eyes. Otherwise how will we see?!

Sirshree : So one answer came as the 'eyes'. The eyes are seeing.

But when are the eyes able to see? A person is dead, his eyes are open, is he able to see? No. That means if the mind is connected to the eyes, then we are able to see. Then I am the mind. Again a question arises that can we see the mind? Have you ever experienced seeing the mind?

Q. 128 : I have seen the mind making excuses.

Sirshree : Yes, you have seen the mind making excuses. Haven't you seen the mind being sad? Don't you see the mind being unhappy? Don't you say that I am being insulted, my mind is upset. When you say *my mind* is sad, then who is the one saying this? Who is that? That definitely cannot be the mind. For instance, somebody says that my pen is not working – it directly implies that I am not the pen. When I can see the pen working or not working, what does this mean? Similarly, you are seeing the mind working, getting suspicious, getting upset, getting unhappy. That indicates that I am not the mind. Then, who is seeing the mind? Try to perceive that – right now, at this very moment.

Q. 129 : The mind is seeing the mind.

Sirshree : Then who is the object and who is the subject or seer? The eyes of the body are seeing the body, then should we accept the eyes as 'I' and say "I am the eyes?" When you see the mind, then what answer do you get regarding who is seeing the mind?

Q. 130 : The brain...?

Sirshree : The brain is a part of the body. The mind uses the brain. Then how can the object see the user? Now, tell me who sees the mind?

Q. 131 : The soul is seeing the mind.

Sirshree : Can you see the soul? You are saying this because you have heard this answer about the soul or are you saying this because you saw the soul? What happened? Or did you experience the soul?

Did you see the soul giving directions to the mind? So, whatever you are telling about the soul, have you heard about it or are you experiencing it?

Q. 132 : I have heard about it. So what are you trying to say?

Sirshree : I am telling you to experience it. The body is getting up, sitting, walking, the mind is becoming happy or sad – this means that you are not the body or the mind. If you are not the body or the mind, then will *you* suffer if something happened to your body or mind? When your pen stops writing, will you get distressed? You will say that the pen has stopped working, let me see what should be done about that. Should it be filled with ink or should the refill be changed? Whatever has to be done, you won't do it sorrowfully, isn't it? Similarly, whatever is happening, is not actually happening with the 'real I' or Self, it is happening with the body and the mind. The seer of the mind is separate and that is who you are. Always remember this. Up till now there was so much effort being put by the body and mind so that some particular thing should happen or some particular thing should not happen, there should not be disappointment, the mind should not be unhappy, why did I do wrong?... Actually, you did not do it at all. When you were feeling that you have done this, then in fact it was the mind saying that 'I' have done this. A thought appears in man's mind that 'I have done this.' What can be a bigger misunderstanding! Here 'I' stands for the body and the mind, and in your speech whenever you have said

'I', you have always meant the body or the mind. However, after attaining the final understanding, when you shall say 'I', then that will be the 'real I'.

If this does occur, then what will happen? How will your life be? You had always believed that this body and mind is 'I', but what will happen if this attachment to your body-mind breaks?

Q. 133 : Then there will be no more misery…?

Sirshree : Even if there is misery, it will be to the mind and body; which was happening earlier too.

Q. 134 : Why does Self need a body and a mind?

Sirshree : Good question! Let us understand it in this manner. When the Self is Self, then there is no need for a body-mind. What will be your answer if you are asked the question that what is the need for a painter to make a painting? Have you ever seen such a painter who has never made a painting?! No. Then we cannot even call him a painter. Likewise, the answer regarding the requirement of a body-mind is that Self is vacuum; which means it is nothing. Now the Self wants to express itself in this vacuum. Take the example of a clay pot. When the walls of the pot are made, then there will be empty space or vacuum inside and outside the pot. Are these two vacuums different? No, they are one and the same. Similarly, if we consider the walls of the pot as our body, and if the question is asked: What part of the pot do we use? Do we use the walls of the pot or the empty space inside the pot? If the potter fills up the entire pot with clay without leaving any empty space inside, then are you going to call that a pot? No.

In the same way, a painter is making a painting to express himself. And is a painter called a painter after making just one painting? He keeps expressing himself by making many varied paintings (bodies).

Q. 135 : But is there any other reason for creating the paintings?

Sirshree : He is creating the paintings for his own joy and for no other reason. His intention behind making these paintings is not to sell them or earn money. All the paintings are the same for him because all paintings are indicating towards the one fact that he is a painter.

Q. 136 : Then what is our body-mind mechanism?

Sirshree : Our body-mind mechanism is the painter's creation or the canvas on which a composition is going to be created. That painter is the Self. But what is going to happen with our body-mind mechanism? There must be some purpose behind the *tejgyan* (knowledge of the ultimate truth) that you are going to attain. Surely, it won't happen without any objective.

Q. 137 : So, is there a purpose to my coming over here?

Sirshree : Let us understand this through an example. There are four children in a house. Out of these four, only one child needs to be told that chocolates have been bought and shown the place where they are kept. That child will be called separately. Why have all those questions been arising in your mind since childhood? What is the reason that you are here today? The mind will feel, 'I have come here.' The mind considers itself to be the 'I'. It feels, 'I have come here. I am listening and I have to understand.' But later on it becomes clear that it was not 'I' who came. Father had to tell someone where the chocolates are kept and hence one was chosen.

There are millions of people. Do such questions occur to all of them? Or even if such questions do arise in them, do they search for the answers? Why do they not look for the answers? And even if they do not, then they are not wrong. It is just that they haven't been chosen for this particular task. Then there is one who begins debating over it, begins to look for the answers through his intellect, in books or by meeting other people. Until he is doing this he feels, "I am doing this." But the day clarity dawns upon him, he realises that 'I' have not done this at all. The body-mind mechanism (BMM) has been imparted a nature that is attuned to such search. For this reason, it was made to seek for answers. The day this is made clear to him, he experiences the Self. After experiencing the Self, duality does not remain. He realises that 'you' and 'I' are not different. If there are four pots, then all the pots contain the same vacuum in them.

Q. 138 : Then, Sirshree, have I been born?

Sirshree : When you realise that that vacuum is 'I', then will you say, "I was born?" You have been saying that you were born on a particular date. But after realising your true nature, you will say, "I haven't been born at all." If I haven't been born at all, then does that mean I won't die?

If you haven't been born, how will you die? Then you are beyond birth and death. See what happens now. What happens after realising the truth? This is similar to what happens to the lead character (actor) of a typical Hindi movie. Just a moment earlier he was singing a song with the love of his life. The very next moment he comes to know that his real mother is someone else. He immediately leaves his mother (whom he had been considering his mother all this time). He did not have to put any effort in leaving this mother. He did not even need to convince himself of anything. In fact, he even left behind the love of his life. He did not even think for a moment about all the promises he had made to her. Everything was left behind and he reached his real mother's home.

Q. 139 : From this, what is it that this BMM will understand?

Sirshree : It will understand how the tongue can taste the tongue. The mind wants to see the Self. The mind wants to be the master of Self and the mind has an ego too. It does not readily accept the truth. The mind says, "I have done this and I have done that." But when suddenly someone tells it that you haven't done anything, it receives a big shock, a big jolt. It says, "How can this be? I have evidence that I have done this."

Q. 140 : Sirshree, now it is becoming clear that we are a painting which has being given the power to think. But we are separate from it.

Sirshree : This is what the mind is feeling. But the mind is an object. What has it done for a question to arise in it? While asleep, did it think, 'Now I should shift sides, otherwise the part laid upon will pain?' Was this happening because of conscious efforts by the mind? No. This was happening automatically.

Q. 141 : What is the subconscious mind?

Sirshree : The inner, instinctive, intuitive mind is the subconscious mind. The role of this mind is to control the involuntary functions of the body (breathing, heartbeat, digestion, automatic responses, etc.). When you are driving a car, if a bicycle comes your way, do you actually think, 'I will now turn left... however, there are children there... Fine, I will turn right... but the car can skid on that side due to a swamp there... so let me apply the brakes.' No. The brakes of the car are applied automatically. Later on you cook up a story saying, "I was driving on the road when somebody suddenly appeared in front of me. I assessed the situation. Some children were playing on the left and the car was likely to skid on the right side. So I applied the brakes." Now this came from memory. Hence the mind felt that I have done it. But did you do it? Or did it just happen? Or you were made to do it?

Q. 142 : It just happened...

Sirshree : Then let it happen even now. Brakes will be applied at the right time by the instinctive mind. But the outer mind feels, 'I have done it.'

Q. 143 : 'I' means who?

Sirshree : Here, 'I' means the outer mind (external mind or contrast mind*). Even if things get done by the instinctive mind, the outer mind feels – I have done it. Which means, we are talking about the ego here. In reality, the outer mind does not do anything. It has believed itself to be the Self. But the Self is far beyond it. For instance, there is a car, a driver, and the owner is sitting at the back. The owner has ordered the driver to go to a particular destination. Now the driver feels he is the master. When he turns right, the car turns right and when he turns left, the car turns left. This creates the illusion in him that he is the owner of the car. But he does not know that he is headed for that destination because the real owner seated at the back has directed him to do so. Now he begins to fear things like, what if he encounters the traffic police? But if he really knew that he is only a driver (an employee), then will he be scared? He will then say, "Let the police come. The owner is right behind." If he has no driving license, then the owner will pay the fine. If there is something to be explained, then the owner will do it. Does the driver have to worry about these things? Does he need to fear about the car breaking down? The owner is there. He will get it fixed. Why should he worry? The car here stands for the body, the driver for the mind, and the owner for the Self. The Self does not do anything directly, everything just happens in its presence.

Q. 144 : Does the Self give orders?

Sirshree : The Self does not issue orders. But orders are passed out and carried out by its mere presence. When the sun rises, the flowers begin to bloom. Does the sun do anything for that? People sleeping inside their homes begin to wake up. But the sun has not even touched them.

Q. 145 : Then what is the Self?

Sirshree : That is what you are.

Q. 146 : But Sirshree, I am the conscious mind, isn't it?

Sirshree : Believing that 'I am the conscious mind' is a great delusion. Hence the question has been raised as to what is the truth? Who are you? After knowing this, there is nothing more that needs to be known.

Q. 147 : Sirshree, is the Self inside the body or outside it?

Sirshree : Everything is inside the Self. Just like all the pots are inside the Self and there is Self inside every pot. There is nothing other than the Self. There is only a curtain in between. The Self is on this side of the curtain as well as on the other. There are small and large holes in the curtain. The Self is in them too. Everything is connected. Everything is the Self alone.

Q. 148 : What is the curtain?

Sirshree : The curtain stands for the identification with the body-mind.

Q. 149 : Who made the Self?

Sirshree : Is there a need to create the Self? It always was and will always continue to be.

Q. 150 : Then what is the brain?

Sirshree : The brain is the tool of the mind and the mind is the tool of the Self. Self means presence. It is just 'being'. This is just like in the presence of the sun and the body, a shadow is cast. No one created this shadow; it just got created on its own.

Q. 151 : Does that mean that the Self is the shadow?

Sirshree : No. The mind is the shadow. It was not created. It got formed. It is an illusion – the biggest illusion.

Q. 152 : Then, doesn't the mind exist?

Sirshree : The existence of the mind is an illusion. Just as an image in a mirror is an illusion. It exists, and yet it does not. Therefore, we have to understand it. The purpose of understanding is that you get stabilised in the absolute silence (*moun*).

*****Contrast Mind :** This is a term coined by Sirshree to indicate the mind that compares, measures and judges everything in dual attributes like good, bad, better, worse, big, small, etc.

Q. 153 : Why is the mind always disturbed?

Sirshree : The thought, 'I do the work' by itself creates disturbance. First understand how work happens. Remember who you actually are and then work will no longer be a burden for you. For every thought that comes naturally, the mind brings its own thoughts on those thoughts. It then stamps its own beliefs and imaginations on those thoughts. Due to this it begins somersaulting into the past and the future. It moves out of the present. This is the trouble with the mind. But as soon as it realises the truth, it stops and becomes calm. Consequently, the bright happiness that was veiled behind the mind is revealed.

Q. 154 : Then how does all work happen? And what is the real thing?

Sirshree : Let us understand this with the example of a cinema screen. The movement of pictures on the screen does not have any effect on the screen per se. The audience pays attention only to the pictures. But the pictures cannot exist without the screen. Yet no attention is paid to the screen. Even if there is a scene of fire in the movie, it cannot burn the screen. Similarly, the fire of anger, jealousy and malice present in man cannot disturb the Self. It is the duty of man to find that unwavering and thoughtless state or seat of being and to take efforts to stabilise therein. Success is assured.

Q. 155 : How do we reach that state of being?

Sirshree : There is a fine curtain of the mind that veils that state. When the mind begins to attain understanding that is imparted at the Final Truth Discourses, that curtain disappears. With the fall or surrender of the mind, that state begins to reveal and manifest on its own. In that state, there is neither joy nor sorrow. Beyond both polarities is the Supreme Silence (*Tej Moun*), the Bright Happiness which man experiences and also wants to share it with others.

Q. 156 : But a movie has an operator?

Sirshree : A movie is played on a lifeless or insentient screen. Hence a conscious being is required to operate it. But the screen or the state present within us is full of consciousness. In fact the screen in essence is Consciousness itself. No other operator is required there.

Q. 157 : Does that mean that work does not get done by our doing? Is everything operated by that state within us? Should we sit idle, doing nothing?

Sirshree : Beliefs regarding deeds and doer either trouble you or set you free. A crow has only one eye to see in both directions. An elephant uses its trunk as a hand as well as a nose. Likewise, whether you believe it or not, there is only one truth. There is only one doer. To attain that state alone is man's ultimate aim. Whether you believe it or not. The doer of doing something (*karma*) or nothing (*akarma*) is one – the Absolute Silence (*moun*), the Self.

Q. 158 : What is *moun*?

Sirshree : *Moun* is the state of absolute silence beyond speech and thought. Words emerge from this silence and also disappear in it. This silence exists between every word, between every thought. It is on the paper of *moun*, that words of thoughts are written. To attain that *moun* alone is to attain the Self. *Moun* is the best language.

Q. 159 : Is it necessary to stay in seclusion?

Sirshree : Seclusion exists inside man. If man is able to maintain complete peace of mind even while dealing with the world, he is actually living in seclusion. The one living by himself in a forest but consumed by thoughts, although alone, is not living in seclusion. Understanding of the truth will easily lead you into seclusion. Seclusion can also be attained easily through meditation. Seclusion stands for the end of one, where there is neither you, nor me, neither two nor one.

Q. 160 : When I sit for meditation, many other thoughts intrude and disturb me.

Sirshree : Yes, during meditation, all kind of thoughts do arise. All the thoughts that are buried inside you, have to come out. If they do not emerge and come face to face with the witness, then how will the mind be annihilated? These thoughts torment us only because we get attached and identified with them. You are the witness of the thoughts. You are not the thoughts.

Knowing (perceiving) and realising the one who is knowing every experience during meditation is Self Realisation.

Q. 161 : How can the Self be experienced?

Sirshree : The experience of the Self is not something external that needs to be regained. It is ever-present from the very beginning. Due to our false identification with the body, we have forgotten the self.

Q. 162 : Are occult powers attained after Self Realisation?

Sirshree : If somebody begins the quest with the motive of attaining occult powers, it means he has gone astray from the path of the real goal. These powers make the mind stronger because such powers are displayed in front of an audience and appreciation is gained from them. This only boosts the ego. Hence, it is inappropriate for the truth seeker to even think of attaining powers. Only the knowledge of the ultimate truth should be your goal.

Q. 163 : Will my Self Realisation benefit others?

Sirshree : Definitely. This is the greatest service. Seeing you, others too will be inspired to attain that ultimate bliss. Due to this desire, they too will become truth seekers and ultimately attain the final knowledge.

Q. 164 : I try a lot and yet I am unable to find that 'I'. How is it? I can't see anything.

Sirshree : You want to know the 'I' through your imagination. The truth is beyond imagination. When the mind is unable to see something, it begins to imagine about it. Instead of imagining, just relax and feel it. However, in order to perceive the sense of your being, you will first have to attain understanding. Otherwise, the mind will time and again spin the web of imagination. Hence, try to reach the root of 'I'.

Q. 165 : How do we reach the root of 'I'?

Sirshree : You can reach the root of 'I' through understanding. This Understanding is imparted in the Final Truth Discourses through which the mind will accept everything and surrender itself to the Self. In this way the mind is eliminated. Self-surrender and understanding is one and the same. When the ego recognises the power of God, it surrenders itself, and with understanding it goes into Silence (*moun*).

Q. 166 : Can we attain understanding through meditation?

Sirshree : No. Meditation is abiding in the truth within. That truth is not to be brought from anywhere. This truth has always been within us and will always be. Attaining the truth is not difficult. After just understanding the false beliefs of our mind, we begin to experience the truth. Hence on attaining understanding, it becomes possible to abide in the truth and this being on the truth is what has been called meditation. It is not that meditation is done only sitting at a place. Once understanding is attained, only meditation will remain in every activity; be it sitting, standing, moving around or doing some work. Hence it is said – Understanding first, meditation later.

Understanding is the seed; Meditation is the fruit.

Truth is the seed; Constant remembrance of God is the fruit.

First know the truth through understanding, and then what remains is just meditation and remembrance of the Lord.

Q. 167 : Sirshree, please tell me some last words that will initiate some contemplation.

Sirshree : During sleep, you do not feel your body. If there is no body, that means the senses of the body are also not functional. Due to which the world too disappears. On rising in the morning, you say, "I had a wonderful sleep." But:

– Who was knowing this in sleep?

– Who was awake?

– Who slept at night? And who remained awake?

– Who awoke in the morning? And who went to sleep in the morning?

– Did it really go to sleep in the morning, or just got concealed by the false beliefs of the mind?

– How do we find that ever-awake witness?

– How do we find the sacred Bright Place (*tejasthan*) within?

– How to attain that state (which was in sleep) even while in the waking state?

Do contemplate on this. "Who am I?" – make this question your meditation. (Refer to chapter 16 to read this meditation in detail).

Then there is freedom from all misery. There is freedom from the vices of the mind. How can the mind that tries to understand everything in the world, become an object itself? How can it surrender? The needless unremitting thoughts of the mind should stop. You should begin to live in the present and become established (stabilised) in your true nature. These are my good wishes or happy thoughts for you.

CHAPTER 12

The Importance of Understanding in Meditation – Part I

Understanding and Listening

Guru   : What is light?
Disciple : Light is the absence of darkness.
Guru   : No.
Disciple : Light is in which we can see everything.
Guru   : Who sees light?
Disciple : The eyes see light.
Guru   : Due to what can the eyes see?
Disciple : Due to the mind and brain.

Guru : Who is seeing the mind and the brain?
Disciple : I don't know.
Guru : That is the real light, in which everything comes into light and everything becomes clear. That alone is Bright (*tej*) light. That is the light of truth. It is beyond light and darkness. Darkness also is a part of that Bright light. What do you see when you close your eyes?
Disciple : Darkness.
Guru : In which light do you see that darkness? That light, in which even darkness is seen, is 'Bright Light'.

Q. 168 : In the retreat, when we were given the exercise to go to the centre of our being (tejasthan, Bright place or heart), I could not see any light there. But while contemplating with my eyes closed, I saw a light. I was able to concentrate on that light and drift into silence and felt immense joy. What does this mean?

Sirshree : The question is that when you reached the centre of being (*tejasthan*), no light was seen. But during contemplation, a light was seen within.

Now understand, in what light did you see that light? A light is needed to see another light. Without that light, this light cannot be seen. When you go within, you find only darkness. You are then asked – in which light did you see the darkness? That 'light' is important. When people forget this, they take the light they see during meditation as an end in itself. If a light is seen, it is a milestone; an indicator to move ahead. A milestone is a stone you see by the roadside, indicating the distance yet to be covered to your destination. But on seeing one, you do not go and sit on the milestone thinking that now I have got the news of my destination, so let me stop right here. Likewise, on getting an indication of your destination by seeing a light, you do not have to stop there. You should say that this milestone is for helping me reach my destination. You saw a light today. Next time always sit with the attitude that you will see what happens next. Do not get stuck with such things. Knowing the light (Bright light) in which light is seen is the true Experience. To get stabilised and permanently abide in that Experience is our ultimate goal.

This mistake is quite often made by those who practise meditation. They consider any light that is seen to be more powerful and significant, and they feel it is the goal. They feel they saw the light, that means they got the result of meditation. However they do not understand that realising the light in which they saw the light is the real goal. If during meditation they do not understand anything and experience deep silence (moun), that silence is the result. But they do not think so. Seeing a light of some kind is perceived as a result. One says, "At least I experienced something", because light is visible but silence cannot be seen. Hence a meditator is constantly warned that only seeing something should not become his goal.

Further the person says, "I went into silence and felt immense joy." Happiness is bound to be experienced. Whenever a new experience occurs within the body, the mind is absent. The mind comes later and expresses its desire for that experience. You saw the light and entered into silence and consequently felt great happiness. But then the contrast mind too turns up and says that it wants the same experience again. Therefore you should have all the information and understanding about the contrast mind too.

Q. 169 : While meditating I feel a strain on the forehead in the beginning, which seems to impede meditation. And till now, I haven't experienced the feeling of the disappearance of the body. Please guide me.

Sirshree : While meditating, a strain is felt in the head because you are putting in a lot of effort. For example, sit up and tense your body. Then try to get sleep by saying, "Let me get sleep…sleep…sleep…" You will not be able to fall asleep. But as soon as you let go and simply lie down without making any effort to get sleep, there is a possibility that you will fall asleep. Similarly, meditation means 'doing nothing'.

Let us understand what we do in meditation. In the quest to attain or seek something, we concentrate our attention and apply strain on the third eye (a spot midway between the eyebrows). Here, the seeker is told, "Stop seeking and completely lose yourself. Only then will the tension be released." This means that when a person focuses his attention upon his heart (*tejasthan*), he is able to sit with ease.

The other question is, why is the disappearance of the body not experienced during meditation? The answer is that you are not meditating in order to make the body disappear. It is true that the feeling of the body disappears during meditation. But you do not need to meditate to experience this feeling. Whether the feeling of the body disappears or not should be of no concern to you. Disappearance of the body implies that the body is not felt. It does not mean that the body will become invisible to others. Others will be able to see your body. It is just that you will not be able to feel it because you will be completely lost in meditation. But remember that you are not meditating to make the feeling of the body disappear. Otherwise, in the pursuit of this experience, the true purpose of meditation will be lost.

It is extremely important to know what meditation is. Meditation is to bring about discipline in our body, to be able to understand: How to attain the desired result? What kind of discipline is needed to attain it? How to control the mind in order to achieve it? Meditation is for attaining this knack. If this understanding is missing, then meditation becomes an wasted meditation or *vyavadhan* (an obstacle to the true purpose). People practise wasted meditation in the name of meditation.

Understand why this is an obstacle. People think that if the feeling of the body disappears, if they see a particular light, then the same should happen the next time too. They meditate with the same expectation. But if at times, the head feels heavy or dizzy or any such feeling crops up, they compare it with their previous experience and feel that their meditation session was not successful. Only when you get the art of seeing meditation in the right perspective, it can be said that you have learnt meditation. Here dizziness, numbness of the limbs or any other such feelings are not of any significance. What is important is whether you saw them from the right perspective. How do you perceive the numbness in your feet? If you think, 'Oh Why have my feet become numb? I had heard that the feeling of the body disappears during meditation. Yet this happened… why?!" If such queries arise, then you have not understood meditation at all.

Have the right understanding. Do not get involved in things such as whether the light was seen or not, whether vibrations were felt in the body or not, whether the nectar was savored or not. Just focus on your primary aim – 'Who am I? What is my aim?' You have to strengthen your conviction regarding the answers to these questions through meditation.

Observe how you prepare to sleep at night by arranging the pillow and the covers, keeping a glass of water at the bedside, having a glass of milk, and so forth. After having made all these preparations, you just relax and lie down on the bed. You do not keep checking if the feeling of the body has disappeared or not, whether you have fallen asleep or not. You know that if you try to check, then whatever little sleep was setting in, will also disappear. Similarly, before sitting to meditate, you make the required preparations such as offering a prayer, sitting in the right posture, etc. But this preparation is not meditation. What is being said is that do put in efforts in preparation. But once done with the preparations, let go of all your efforts and desires to see light, to lose the feeling of the body, etc.

Q. 170 : What is understanding?

Sirshree : Whenever a seeker sets out on the path of truth, the first question that arises in his mind is, 'What is understanding? Can Self Realisation be attained merely by listening? Can the ultimate experience be attained by just being present in the Final Truth discourses – the experience in the quest of which so many seekers get entangled in various paths?' On the path of listening and understanding, the seeker can easily attain the answers to the questions – 'Who am I?', 'What is the essence of my being?' at the experiential level. Out of all the paths that have been propounded, the path of understanding is the best. This is because while following the paths of *japa* (chanting), *tapa* (penance and austerities), *tantra* (mystical practices), *mantra, karma* (deeds), religion, devotion, meditation and knowledge, as long as understanding is not associated, these paths will not take the seeker to that supreme goal. Hence understanding has the highest importance in spirituality. Any seeker, who sets out on any path without understanding, will not be able to reach the final goal. 'Understanding' alone is complete in itself. Listening is the most important thing on this path. Hence it has also been called the 'ear path'. Hence it is of utmost importance that man learns the art of right listening.

Q. 171 : What is right listening through which one attains understanding?

Sirshree : Right listening is listening to even those words which are being spoken behind the words, due to which one begins to go within onto his essential being and begins recognising his true self. Hence, knowledge of words is not real knowledge, because how can words express the absolute silence? Words lead us up to that silence, that is their aim. But the knowledge of words can confuse the seekers. Hence, initially that entity will be expressed through words alone, as there is no other available method. The source of all words is that silence. One needs to stabilise in that silence, and become free from words. Otherwise people use these words of knowledge to demonstrate their knowledge. The ultimate goal of knowledge is to take you to the state of absolute silence. One throws away the ice candy stick after having eaten the ice candy. The ice candy is that state and the stick signifying the words was instrumental in bringing about that state. Hence it is absolutely essential to know the true art of listening.

Q. 172 : Does that mean that our everyday listening is not right listening?

Sirshree : This question arises in everybody's mind: 'What is right listening? We do listen every day.' However, this is not the listening due to which the head becomes heavy. Right listening is that due to which one is liberated from the head. It is freedom from the head, because every person is tormented by the countless thoughts that arise in the head. Thoughts are of two types – negative thoughts and positive thoughts. It is not possible to be liberated from all thoughts in the beginning itself. Therefore, begin by converting negative thoughts into positive thoughts. There are countless negative thoughts churning in the head throughout the day. Due to these, a negative mindset is formed and one faces many problems as a result of that. Once a negative mindset is formed, one always tends to extract something negative even out of something totally positive. Once you are free from negative thoughts, you need to attain freedom from positive thoughts too. This happens automatically through 'understanding'. This is the simplicity of this path – you can attain freedom from thoughts just by listening. Otherwise, a seeker tries all his life to get free from the bondage of thoughts, but is never successful. In this path, you only need to listen and understand. To attain freedom from thoughts is to attain freedom from the mind. The mind is just a bundle of thoughts. The mind (contrast mind) is that which divides in two, compares, judges and measures. Comparing is to say, "This is good, that is bad." Comparison always divides into two polarities and puts two kinds of labels on each and every thing. But this contrast mind falls spontaneously through understanding and then it begins thinking even about the thoughtless.

CHAPTER 13

The Importance of Understanding in Meditation – Part II

GOD AND I

There is a home within your home. Meditation is entering that home within. Every night you leave the market and come into your neighborhood. Then you leave your neighborhood and come into your home. After sitting in the hall, you go into your bedroom. Leaving the bedroom, you go onto the bed. Leaving the bed, closing the eyes, you go onto the body. Then finally, leaving the body you enter the home within and sleep in comfort. Meditation is resting and rejoicing consciously in that inner home.

Q. 173 : Does God exist?

Sirshree : An atheist will say, "God does not exist" and a theist or a believer will say, "God exists." Both have incomplete knowledge. The truth is: *Only God exists.* Whether God exists or not, is itself a wrong question. A person is lying on the bed and somebody asks him, "Are you awake?" If he says, "Yes," you understand that he is awake. But if he says, "No," it still means that he is awake. In the same way, if one says that God exists, it means God exists and if one says that God does not exist, it still means that God exists. Even to be able to say "No," that body has to have the presence of God within it. Now you have understood that only God exists because who is saying "no"? It is Him alone. 'God alone exists. Find out and ascertain whether you exist.' You believe yourself to be separate from everybody and everything. Are you really separate?

Q. 174 : What is the name of God?

Sirshree : 'Nameless Truth' is the name of God. It is a fact that all names are the names of God or no name is the name of God. All forms are the forms of God or no form is the form of God. Whenever someone has proclaimed the truth to this world, he has chanted the name of God. Simply chanting out 'Om, Om' or 'Krishna, Krishna' is not true chanting. The truth that was chanted even before the word 'Om' was created is the name of God. The truth that was chanted even before the birth of Krishna is the name of God. The truth that was chanted before the birth of Jesus is the name of God. Truth is God and God is the truth. The name chanted by Rama, the son of Dasharatha, is the name of God. The name chanted by Krishna, the son of Devaki, is the name of God. The name chanted by Jesus, the son of Mary, is the name of God.

---

*Ravana: The name of the demon in the epic Ramayana, whom Lord Rama slays in the end. He can be considered to be the embodiment of all the vices of the mind.

If 'Nameless Truth' is the name of God, then just chanting "Truth, Truth" will also not be true chanting. Only when you 'think the truth', does true chanting take place. 'Thinking the truth' and 'thinking about the truth' are two different things. When you are reading stories of Rama, Krishna, Jesus, Mohammad the Prophet, etc., you are 'thinking about the truth', not 'thinking the truth'. If during the night, someone states, "It is night now," then in spite of it being true, it is not 'the truth'. The understanding with which the name of God was considered to be the truth is not this truth. To chant the truth or to think the truth is to think 'Who am I' and to constantly remember who the actual doer of all deeds is. Learn the right method of remembering the name of God from the right Guru and chant the name of God.

All names are the names of God or no name is the name of God. All forms are the forms of God or no form is the form of God. Uttering the name that takes you to the experience of your being is the name of God. Even on uttering 'Rama', if you are reminded of the illusory world (*maya*), then it is not the name of God. On the contrary, by uttering the name 'Ravana'*, if you are reminded of the truth, then that is the name of God.

Q. 175 : What is the significance of pictures or idols of God?

Sirshree : God is formless and beyond the mind and intellect. Man uses his mind and intellect to understand everything. It is essential to use pictures to teach a child. What pictures need to be shown to the beginners in spirituality? No picture can be made of God. But considering the requirement, this deliberate mistake of making pictures or idols of God was made by men of realisation. This mistake gets rectified on attaining God. God needs a form to know Himself, just as an eye needs a mirror to see itself.

Q. 176 : Does God have a form or is He formless?

Sirshree : A new truth seeker cannot understand this and so he is asked two questions:

1. Does God have a form and sometimes becomes formless?
   Or
2. Is God formless and can take form when He wants to?

The second answer is the right answer. What would a person with an ordinary intellect give more importance to – gold or gold ornaments? To the ornaments. But in all these ornaments there is only one thing common… and that is gold. When gold is given form and shape, its value increases in the material world. Similarly, people give more importance to form. But for the goldsmith, gold or gold ornaments are one and the same. A goldsmith sees gold in every gold ornament. The shape of the ornaments and the shapelessness of raw gold is the same thing for him. Likewise, to the one with understanding of the truth and God, form and formless are the same.

People who believe in form and the ones who believe in the formless are both watching the same movie. Some are watching the part of the movie before the interval and some are watching the part after the interval. After watching the movie, when they get a chance to meet each other, they argue saying, "You are wrong." But the fact is that both of them have seen the same movie. Formless is the form of God, 'no attribute' is the attribute of God.

Q. 177 : Where is God?

Sirshree : You can choose one from the three answers given below:

1. God is only within us.
2. God is everywhere in the world outside us.
3. God is both inside and outside.

From the three answers given above, which do you think is the right one? You may feel that either the first answer or the third answer is the right one. But in reality, God is beyond inside and outside. Inside and outside is the language of the mind. God is beyond the reach of mind and hence God is beyond inside and outside, i.e. God is everywhere. Now if God is both inside and outside, the question arises where is He easier to find? It is easier to find God within us because our body is with us all twenty-four hours of the day. We can take a dip within, whenever we like. At the same time, we are also within God, just like fish in water.

Q. 178 : How is God?

Sirshree : Different answers can be given to this question. One can be – God is nothing and the world was created out of nothing. An entire forest is contained within a seed. But when you break a seed and look inside it, what do you find? Nothing. In the same way, God is nothing. But this nothing is not the nothing which the mind usually conceives. This 'nothing' is everything.

A man arrived at a kingdom. He began telling people strange and unheard things about God. People got upset with what he said. They caught him and took him to the king and said, "This man has been talking strangely about God."

When asked for an explanation, the man said to the king, "I can prove that I am not misguiding people." To prove his point he called three ministers and gave a packet of soil or earth to each one of them. Then he said to them, "Describe what is in this packet without mentioning its name."

The first minister said, "Everything is born out of this. It is such a thing from which everything is created. The seeds of all plants, shrubs and trees are within it."

The second one said, "This is not water. Apart from water, whatever remains, it is that thing."

The third one said, "It is that into which everyone will finally merge."

The man then revealed the purport of the experiment saying, "Even when asked about a simple thing like the soil or earth, you get three different answers. Imagine how many different answers can then be given about God? So if the answer is different, does it change the entity in any way?" The king was convinced. Are you convinced too?

God is the consciousness, the life within us. The fact is God cannot be described in words, He can only be experienced. God is that 'nothing' which has the potential of everything.

Q. 179 : Who created God?

Sirshree : Do you think God can die?

Seeker : No, definitely not.

Sirshree : Then can something that cannot die, be ever created? Only that which is born can die. When anyone asks you this question, ask him in return, "Does God die?" He will say, "No." (How can God die?) If God does not die, then how can he be born? God is beyond the cycle of birth, death, time and imagination. Only that dies which is born. God is the 'Bright Life' beyond life and death, that life which has no end.

Q. 180 : Then when did God, who is unborn, create this world?

Sirshree : "When was this world created?" – this question has to do with time. But the concept of time came after the world was created. How is it then possible to give an answer using a concept that came later? Or understand it in this way – time began when the world got created. How can that, which was before time, be brought within the frame of time? What was before time is actually what is important. That, which was before time, always existed, continues to exist and will always exist. Time is just a small part of it. A part can never measure the whole. God is samadhi (*samay* = time, *aadhi* = before), which means before time began. The world was created when time had not been created yet.

Q. 181 : Where did God come from?

Sirshree : This sounds like a good question. But when you think over it, it signifies that God was elsewhere and not here earlier. And when He came here, then He will not be there where He came from. So, does God keep moving from one place to another? The reality is that God is everywhere (omnipresent). The question, "Where did God come from?" is baseless in itself. If someone asks you, "Is red colour crooked or straight?", you would say that red colour has nothing to do with being crooked or straight – this question is wrong. Similarly questions like, where did God come from? Where was He before that?... are unfounded and therefore pointless to ponder over.

Q. 182 : Can the mind know God?

Sirshree : God is beyond the mind. The mind will never be able to know God. When the mind becomes still, only then is God manifested. But the mind can never accept that there can be any such thing that it cannot know. Sometimes people feel embarrassed to admit that they do not know. If we do not know something, then we should say, "I don't know." However, people give some absurd answers in order to avoid embarrassment.

For example, a person fails to attain success despite working very hard for it. He seeks a reason for his failure from someone. The answer he receives is: "It is because of your bad luck that you could not succeed." Another person tells him, "You must have committed certain bad deeds in your last birth. Hence success eludes you now." Thus, instead of saying, "I don't know," readymade answers are given related to luck, destiny or previous births. We should not be embarrassed to say "I don't know." It does not make any difference when we admit this.

When a child asks a question to his father and the father does not know the answer, the father should say, "Come on son. Let us look for the answer together."

A person asks his friend, "Why do we find dew drops on leaves in the morning?" His friend replies, "The Earth perspires as it has to rotate the whole day… this sweat is seen on the leaves." Here too, instead of saying, "I don't know," some ridiculous answer is given.

In this way readymade answers are handed out such as destiny, heaven and hell, the result of deeds from past births, etc. If this birth were the result of karma (deeds) from past lives, then what was the cause of the first birth? Due to which karma would the first birth have taken place? Man is just scared to admit that he does not know and continues to dish out speculative answers. It is due to such answers that many imaginary and erroneous images and concepts of God have developed. The mind can imagine about God; however, it cannot experience God. The eyeglasses can never see the eyes. The mind is the eyeglass of God. Hence the mind can never see God. When the mind becomes a 'no-mind' through contemplation and understanding, only then does God manifest.

Q. 183 : Is God a male? Are the pictures of God imaginary?

Sirshree : God is beyond gender and imagination.

One day a teacher asked a student, "How is the sky?" The student answered, "The sky is yellow", for he had seen the sky at dusk. A second student replied, "The sky is black", because he had seen the sky at night. If we are asked the same question, we might say that the sky is blue.

Similarly, a picture is formed in our minds as soon as someone utters the word 'God'. People who have been brought up in the Hindu tradition imagine a male God wearing a crown and many ornaments on his body. Similarly, followers of Christianity imagine God in the form of Jesus of Nazareth. This applies to many different religious traditions around the world. Such imaginations too become an obstacle in the quest for God.

We imagine about God too. The belief has set in that God is male. We get entangled in our own beliefs and imaginations. If someone were to ask you, how does a doughnut look like, a ring shape pops up before your eyes. Never a square shape. If a square doughnut is made, will its taste change? No. But our idea is so firm about it that we feel that a doughnut *has to be* ring-shaped. Similarly, we imagine that God has to be male. If any of his embodiments have been depicted in a movie or a television serial by an actor, then that actor's face appears before our eyes. Many such male images of God appear printed on calendars and posters too. A quest based on such imaginary ideas can never attain fulfillment.

Children in kindergarten are taught words. Along with words, pictures of the corresponding objects are also shown. The child learns the words by associating them with pictures. Looking at the pictures, his understanding increases, and in the future he is able to understand the words even without the pictures. Initially, pictures of God are useful. Moving ahead, one can experience God even without pictures. Those who advance from kindergarten spirituality, realise that God is beyond form. God is – eternal, timeless, unborn, self-existent, impregnable, constant, egoless, formless, without attributes, fearless, devoid of enmity, omnipresent, omnipotent, omniscient, spaceless, beyond the senses and beyond the reach of the mind.

Q. 184 : Is it necessary to fear God? Does God get angry?

Sirshree : Fear of God is unnecessary. It is because of imaginations about God that the fear got created. Fear of God was used in society to get everyone to perform good deeds. However, what is the worth of the work done due to the fear of God? Good deeds should arise not out of fear, but out of understanding, love, reverence and respect for God.

The meaning of 'God' is 'love' and love can never be displeased. Out of ignorance, man believes that if he passes by a temple and forgets to fold his hands in reverence, then God will be displeased. This is because man imagines God to be like himself too. If God were to get angry, then what would be the difference between God and man? In a lighter vein, one may say, "God does get angry about the fact that man believes that God gets angry." Fear of God is ignorance, prayer to God is knowledge, love for God is supreme knowledge.

Q. 185 : Who am I?

Sirshree : There is that 'I' which people think you are. There is the 'I' that you consider yourself to be. There is the 'I' which you want to become in the future. All these are false concepts. Actually you are beyond all these. You are not what others perceive you to be. You are not what you perceive yourself to be. The one who perceives within you is the real you. Know that perceiver and you shall know the Self, the God. You are not to know this through words. You can know it only by being it – not by being the body or by being the mind.

Q. 186 : I am not this body, I am not this mind. Then who am I?

Sirshree : You are the one who is asking "Who am I?" You are the 'asker' and once you have realised this, the Oscar Award is yours. If you wish to know, "If I am not all of this, then who am I?", then ask yourself, "Who is it that is asking this?" If you will 'know' this from within, then you will get the real answer. "Who am I" is not a question. It is the answer. People realise this after a long time of enquiry into their true identity. After all, who would want to ask this question? Would the body want to ask, "Who am I?" It knows very well what it is. Even the mind need not know who it is. The intellect too does not want to know who it is. The one who has the desire to know is the real you. That is why the question should actually be, "Who is the asker?"

*Nobody can make you thoughtless
because you have always been thoughtless.*

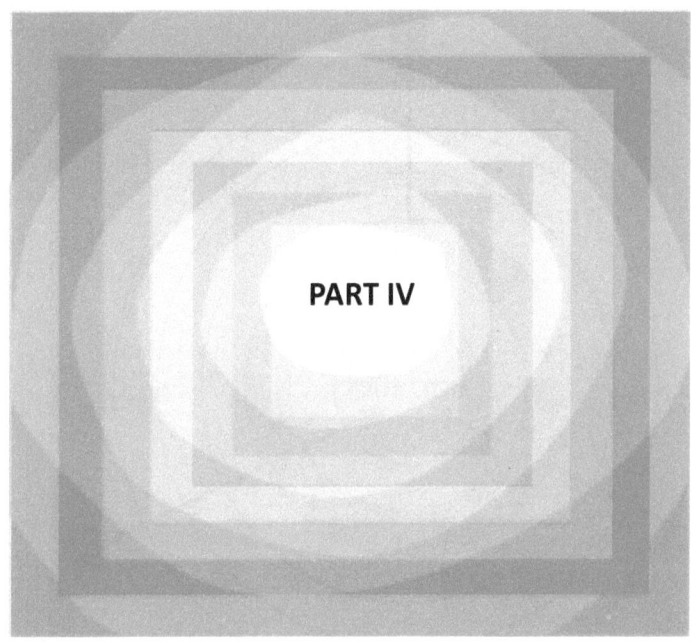

PART IV

MEDITATION FOR MEDITATORS

Meditator (*sadhak*) is a seeker whose quest has come into action; who has begun his spiritual practice. In order to know the answers at the experiential level which he has already understood through the intellect, the disciple journeys ahead through *sadhana* (spiritual practice). It is then that he is called a *sadhak* or meditator. A meditator is one who is able to experience his answers by practising in depth. A meditator is ready to listen directly to the truth.

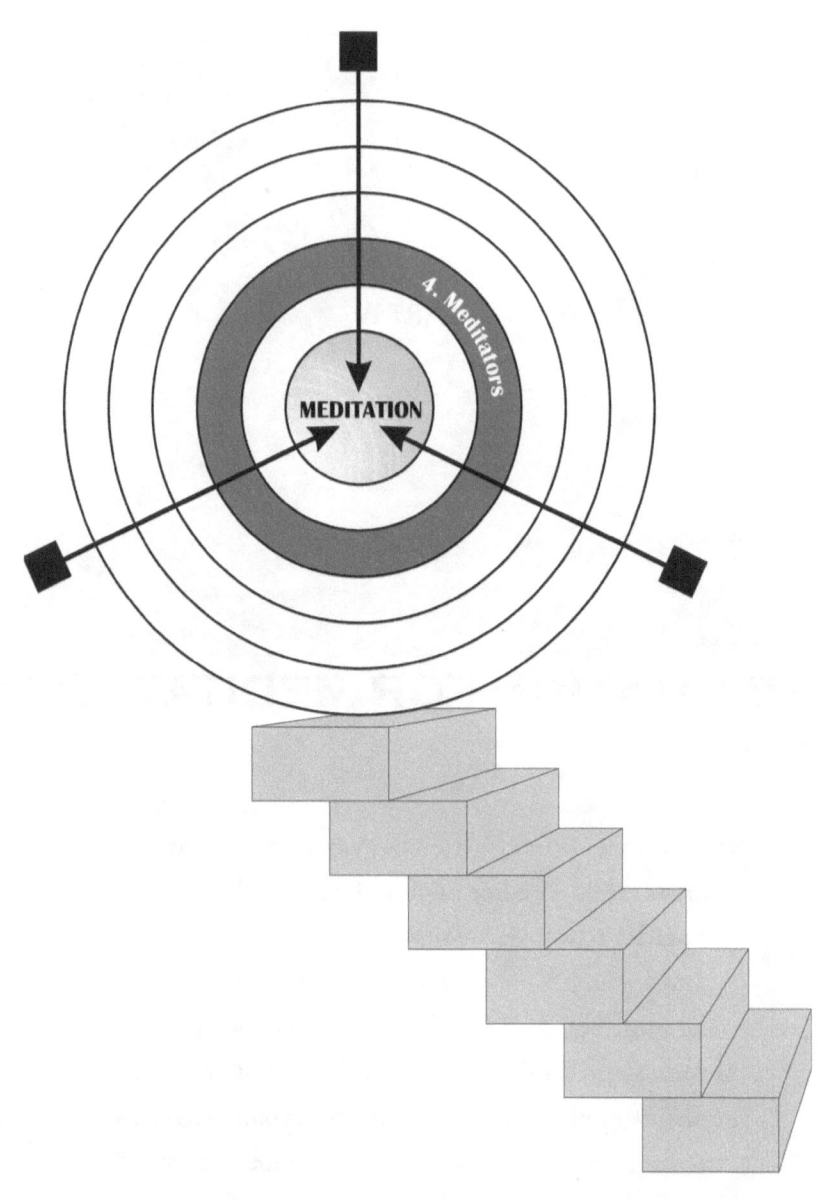

CHAPTER 14

Self Meditation and Wasted Meditation

TECHNIQUES AND OBSTRUCTIONS

A mind filled with reverence can dive into meditation and fall in an instant. Or else, gradually go on emptying the mind. The mind is filled with desires, beliefs and imaginations. As soon as these disappear, you will attain the wealth of 'Self Meditation'.

Q. 187 : What is Self Meditation?

Sirshree : Before understanding Self Meditation, let us understand what is *vyavadhan* (wasted meditation, the obstacle).

Till today, whoever has attained Self Realisation has remained in meditation; which signifies that meditation returned onto itself (Self Meditation). People thought they attained Self Realisation because they practised meditation. But the fact is exactly the opposite. The Buddha remained in meditation after discovering the Self (the truth). It was not that he discovered the Self due to practising meditation. But people insisted, "Tell us too how to meditate? Which techniques should be adopted for meditation?" Hence, for the sake of explanation, they were told:

– Meditate on your body.

– Watch your breath going in and coming out.

– Focus on your breathing. When you focus on this you will realise that you are alive.

This is how people came to know about the technique of breathing.

Q. 188 : Sirshree, I understood about meditation through the breathing technique. But I failed to understand the statement about being alive?

Sirshree : This is not something that can be explained. It has to be experienced. That is why people found it difficult to understand. Hence, they were told, "Okay. Just focus on your breathing." That is how man has continued doing the same till date. The problem with suggesting the technique of focusing on the body is that even till today people are stuck with the physical techniques because a human body is a wonder in itself – in fact, the greatest wonder of the world.

Q. 189 : How can the body be a wonder? What is its relation to meditation?

Sirshree : Meditating on the body, the concentration power of the mind increased. As the mind became more focused, miraculous powers of a focused mind began to be discovered. This in turn led to the realisation that all kinds of miraculous powers could be achieved through a focused mind. This is because while grasping many things, a focused mind can also grasp such things which normally a mind cannot. A focused mind can see things the eye cannot see. An ordinary mind will not be able to see beyond a wall due to physical limitations of the eye. A focused mind can hear sounds that an ordinary mind cannot.

Having discovered the benefits of a focused mind, people did begin meditation. But that meditation became an obstruction or a wasted meditation.

WASTED MEDITATION – AN OBSTRUCTION

Q. 190 : How did meditation become wasted meditation?

Sirshree : Wasted meditation means an obstruction, a hurdle. The primary purpose behind teaching meditation was Self Realisation – knowing the ultimate truth. Man had begun meditation towards attaining this goal alone and not for achieving mystical powers.

Let us understand this through an example. There was a hermitage of a Guru right in the middle of a forest. There was no proper path to reach the hermitage. Additionally, there was a swamp on the way. The Guru used to teach how to walk using stilts to all those disciples who wished to come to the hermitage. (Stilts are two stout poles with foot rests in the middle, used for walking high above the ground). This was taught in various ways. Initially, the disciples used to fall off quite often. But they were made to continue practising. With regular practice, they gradually learnt to walk using stilts. Now the uneven terrain or the swamp was no longer an obstacle for them. They could now easily reach the hermitage.

However, at this juncture, many disciples became content after learning to walk, and forgot their original purpose, which was to reach the hermitage. They were happy to just walk on stilts. Only those disciples who reached the hermitage and showed readiness to listen to the truth were given further knowledge. Being able to walk using stilts was only a preparation. The true aim was Self Realisation. Meditation techniques too are merely a preparation to move towards Self Meditation.

Q. 191 : Are mystical powers the only reason for meditation becoming a hurdle?

Sirshree : Yes. With meditation, there are such powers that begin to awaken in man which make him satisfied with these powers alone. Thus man loses his way and forgets that he had originally begun with the intention of finding that truth, knowing which a person remains in constant meditation and bliss.

Meditation is easy and natural for the one in Self Meditation. However, others are under the delusion that he is meditating to achieve something, he is doing something extraordinary, he is strongly disciplining the mind... But it is not so. Instead, what appears to be penance to others is a pleasure to him. He is experiencing the Self and that experience is so beautiful that he does not need to be reminded to meditate. He will say, "I am already in Self Meditation." He will say the same thing whenever asked to meditate. This means that meditation is our basic quality, our innate nature; we do not have to make an effort to do it. Effort is required to become something that we are not, to attain what we do not have. Being what we already are is effortless.

Q. 192 : Why have you referred to meditation as 'Self Meditation'?

Sirshree : The meaning of the word 'meditation' has been corrupted due to people misunderstanding meditation to be concentration. A person begins with the body and attains high level of concentration. He was told to meditate on the body because it was his desire. The primary purpose behind the exercise was to reach the state of Self Meditation and not get stuck in the techniques of meditation. For this reason, it has been specified as 'Self Meditation.'

Many a time, on seeing pictures of sages and saints sitting in meditation, it is misunderstood that they are in Self Meditation. From external appearance, one can never tell whether a person is meditating or is in Self Meditation. Many people sit with closed eyes. Externally, they may appear to be in Self Meditation. It is possible that internally they are plotting something or are filled with various thoughts or possibly wanting to attain powers. To an external observer, they may appear to be in samadhi. In such a case, the individual ego (the entity within us which assumes a separate existence from the rest of creation) is only becoming stronger.

Q. 193 : How does the individual (one who possesses the individual ego) become strong?

Sirshree : An individual wants to use the power he has attained.

– He wants to prove himself to the world.
– He wants to avenge the people who had troubled him.
– He likes powers so much that he wants to experiment with them as soon as possible.
– He wants to earn a name for himself.

It is not only difficult but impossible for such a person to practise meditation or to attain the Experience of the Self.

In ancient times, the eligibility of a disciple was first evaluated by the Guru, so as to check the purity of mind before imparting the knowledge of powers to him. It was first made sure that he will not misuse these powers.

Q. 194 : What does purity of mind mean?

Sirshree : Purity of mind signifies such a mind that has become pure before surrendering. It is a mind which is filled with goodness;

a mind which has only feelings of well-being of others and can cause no harm to others. An oath used to be taken from the disciples in the ancient times that any power they attained would not be used for wrong purposes. They were taught patience to make their mind anger-free. Otherwise if someone upset them, they would simply put a curse on the other person; and those curses did actualise in those times. Hence they were taught purity of mind right from the beginning, so that when their powers awakened, they could control them and not harm anybody.

But it is always attempted by a true guru to shift people from meditation towards Self Meditation. Meditation should return on itself, wherein 'the experiencer experiences the experiencer'. This implies that the one who is experiencing, experiences the experiencer. Such is the state of Self Meditation. But this cannot be understood until people are actually in Self Meditation. It cannot be understood if they are involved in attaining powers.

Q. 195 : I have seen many people meditating. Aren't they actually meditating?

Sirshree : The word 'meditation' has become so clichéd, that anyone sitting with eyes closed is assumed to be in meditation. But the fact is that there are very few who actually meditate (i.e. who are in Self Meditation). Self Meditation is not possible without knowing the ultimate truth. In the beginning one was told to meditate for attaining the primary aim of Self Realisation. Meditation was utilised as a preparation for the main journey. Though people did get prepared for the journey, they got trapped in the swamp of various techniques. They went astray in the jungle of these techniques and meditation thus became an obstacle. What was meant to be Self Meditation thus became wasted meditation. The true aim of meditation was forgotten. This is akin to polishing your shoes for a journey but never embarking on it.

Q. 196 : What is the main cause of forgetting our true aim?

Sirshree : Beliefs! Beliefs are those notions which the mind assumes to be true, but which are not true. They appear to be true because all people around us believe them to be so. Seeing everyone else believing them, we too begin to believe the same.

When you look through the eyeglasses of such beliefs, everthing appears distorted. 80% of our assumptions prove to be wrong. Bright Light is needed to eliminate the darkness of these beliefs. Bright (*tej*) Light is that which is beyond light and darkness. It is that light in which even darkness is seen. When you close your eyes, you see darkness. In which light do you see this darkness? A kind of light is needed even to perceive darkness. That light is always available within us. It is just that no one has pointed towards it.

Someone then points out, "Meditate on the one who is meditating." Thereby the mistakes that were occurring during meditation are eliminated. Consequently, both light and darkness are experienced. The external light is then seen in the internal light.

MEDITATION AND CONTRAST MIND

Q. 197 : Are there any other hurdles besides false beliefs in reaching the state of Self Meditation?

Sirshree : The biggest obstacle in reaching Self Meditation is the contrast mind. The contrast mind is that which divides everything into two. It compares and comments, 'This is good; that is bad.' It thrives on comparison and judgment. It is due to this that misery exits. Otherwise, 'misery' is not misery. It is the contrast mind that stands blocking the vision of the Experience of Being, giving the impression that there is no Experience. The Bright Knowledge imparts understanding to the contrast mind so that it shuts up and calms down because the mind always wants to see the Experience, which is not possible. The eyeglasses can never see the eyes. Similarly, the Experience can never be felt in the presence of the contrast mind. Let us understand this obstruction caused by the contrast mind through an example.

The contrast mind is like the weeds that cover the surface of water, due to which the reflection of the moon is not visible in the water. If you want to see the reflection of the moon in the water, it is essential that the weeds be cleared. Even after the weeds are cleared, if the surface of the water is not still due to the ripples or waves in it, the moon appears fragmented or distorted. It is to calm these waves that techniques and concentration come of use which allow us to feel the Experience. Here it can be understood that the moon signifies the Self and the weeds stand for the contrast mind.

Q. 198 : How is the contrast mind formed?

Sirshree : The first thought that arises within us when we wake up in the morning is the 'I' thought:

— I awoke

— I arose

— Now what is the first thing that I should do?

— My eyes are a bit heavy today

— Is it time for me to wake up?

The words may vary, but all of them pertain to 'I'. It is with the advent of the 'I' thought that all other thoughts follow. By then, the senses are awake too. It is only after the 'I' thought that the contrast mind forms. The contrast mind then judges everything as 'this is good' or 'this is bad'. The contrast mind survives by assuming a separate identity for itself – my work, my name, my deeds, my religion, my country, my sins, my good deeds. By comparing and contrasting every incident and every thought, the contrast mind fluctuates between joy and sorrow. This alone is the cause of unhappiness and bondage. This alone is the ocean of ignorance. This alone is the illusion. This alone is the obstacle in attaining the truth. This alone is the black cloud shrouding the sun (Self). This alone is the eclipse. This alone is the speck that gets into the eye and stops you from seeing even a mountain.

MEDITATION AND LIGHT

Q. 199 : What is the relation between the internal light and the external light?

Sirshree : The internal light has no relation or connection with the external light. However, gradually people began to get stuck up with words, due to which the misunderstanding began. For instance, if the word 'light' was said for the experience of being, many interpretations got associated with it. Kabir (a saint in India) proclaimed, "The light is like a thousand suns have lit up." One who has known the experience cannot express it in better words and therefore associates it with the sun. The same language that we usually speak is used even after realisation. The experience of being is indescribable, but when asked about it, some words have got to be used. But those who have not yet known the truth cannot think beyond the physical realm. This is the problem with language. The language that is used by the realised ones is always according to the one who is questioning (the seeker). The experience will be described as a lamp, a candle, the sun, the moon and other related entities. How else can they express it? Therefore, when Kabir mentioned 'light', people literally started searching and trying to find light (in a physical sense) within themselves. And they do perceive some light!

Q. 200 : How is the light seen? Some people also see deities. How is that so?

Sirshree : When the mind is concentrated, anything can be seen. And what can be seen, that can speak too. People feel happy that Lord Krishna came to them and even spoke to them. They say, "Today I had a conversation with Lord Shiva. Lord Shiva told me that..." However, what they do not realise is that it was their own mind speaking to them. This was the power of the concentrated mind. But this power by itself became an obstacle in the path of meditation. It became a wasted meditation. A Hindu always sees Hindu deities like Krishna or Rama. He never sees Jesus. A Christian sees Jesus and never Rama or Krishna. Thus, this is all a game of the mind and its beliefs.

TECHNIQUES OF MEDITATION

Q. 201 : How many techniques are there for meditation? Which of them are the more prominent ones?

Sirshree : Today, thousands of people are seen practising meditation. Around 112 techniques of meditation have been described depending on the constitution of the person:

- For those with keen ears, the technique of sound was recommended in which they need to grasp the gap between two sounds.
- For those with keen eyes, there is a different technique.
- For those with an active imagination, there is a different technique.
- Those with a sensitive tongue can reach the Experience through taste.
- Those with sensitive skin can grasp even the minutest sensation through their body.
- For those with keen ears and a keen nose, a different technique was described.
- For those with weak ears, there was a different technique.

In this way a total of 112 techniques were created. If meditation techniques were to be divided into broad categories, they would be:

1) Scientific techniques
2) Spiritual techniques

SCIENTIFIC TECHNIQUES

Scientific techniques are those in which scientific equipments are utilised. These equipment indicate the frequency (alpha, beta, theta, delta) of the brain waves at a particular time. The frequency of the alpha waves is 7-14 cycles/second. In this state, a person experiences a state similar to that of samadhi. Hence it has been called as alpha meditation.

The different types of scientific techniques are:

1) Alpha meditation
2) Hypno meditation
3) Visual meditation

SPIRITUAL TECHNIQUES

Some of the main techniques among them are:

1) 'Who am I' Meditation
2) Beyond Feelings Meditation
3) Thought Witnessing Meditation
4) Breathing Meditation
5) Vipassana Meditation
6) Eagle Meditation
7) Listening Meditation
8) Light Meditation
9) Chakras Meditation
10) Dream Meditation
11) Heart Meditation
12) Navel Meditation
13) Walking Meditation
14) Soham Meditation
15) Mantra Meditation
16) Yoga Meditation
17) Zen Koan Meditation
18) Sound Meditation
19) Sitting Meditation

20) Whirling or Sufi Meditation
21) Holy Sound Meditation
22) Faceless Meditation

Q. 202 : What is the original purpose of all these techniques?

Sirshree : The original purpose was to go beyond (transcend) the body. If you can understand and attain this without any techniques, if you are ready to directly listen and understand, then the path of listening is very easy. With techniques, there is always the danger of the individual (mind, intellect, ego) becoming stronger or getting trapped by mystical powers (*siddhis*). Man does not even realise when his path gets diverted elsewhere. The journey was from meditation towards Self Meditation, i.e. from concentration to meditation. But one does not realise as to when this journey deviated towards the objective of attaining mystical powers.

Q. 203 : Is meditation a path or the destination?

Sirshree : Meditation is the destination, not the path, with the help of which we can elevate the level of our consciousness. But many regard meditation as a path and get lost in the journey of meditation. Someone needs to remind us again that 'meditation' is the final understanding, the aim of which is to know the Self. But if we just keep practising meditation without reaching the Experience, it is like sharpening the edge of a sword all our life, but never going to battle.

Q. 204 : Sirshree, what is the biggest advantage of meditation?

Sirshree : There are many benefits of meditation. But the most significant one is understanding the answer to the most important question, 'Who am I?' The practice of meditation will have served its purpose only if one obtains the answer to this through meditation. This means that meditation is successful only when Self Meditation is attained. To realise the answer to 'Who am I?', the 'Who am I Meditation' should be done which you can read in chapter 16 of this book.

MEDITATION – A SURVEY

A survey was carried out on the subject of meditation. The results of the survey (in percentage) are indicated below:

What is the definition of meditation according to you?

1)	Don't know	10%
2)	Chanting the name of God	40%
3)	Watching thoughts	12%
4)	To calm or concentrate the mind	12%
5)	Contemplation / Reflection	3%
6)	Purification of the mind	3%
7)	Others: to work / attention / to be immersed in the Self with total submission without interference from the outer world/to forget oneself and meditate upon the entire world	20%

Do you meditate?

1)	Yes	55%
2)	No	40%
3)	Sometimes	5%

What types of meditation techniques do you practise?

1)	Dynamic	10%
2)	Yoga	15%
3)	Soham	10%
4)	SSY	10%
5)	Others: *Kundalini / Vipassana / Swadhyaya / Upasana / Rieki /* Reading religious texts/ Reciting mantras	55%

When do you meditate?

1)	Morning	55%
2)	Evening	15%
3)	Night	15%
4)	Any time	10%
5)	When alone	5%

In which posture do you meditate?

1)	Standing	30%
2)	Sitting	40%
3)	Lying down	10%
4)	In any posture	10%
5)	*Padmasana* / Lotus posture	5%
6)	Others	5%

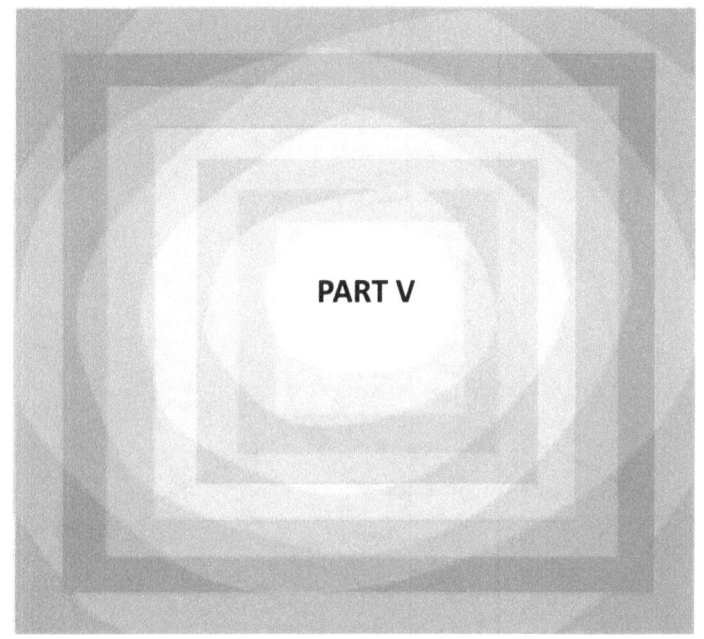

PART V

MEDITATION FOR DEVOTEES

A devotee is the one who is a lover of the truth. A lover of the truth is one who has tasted the truth, who has acquired an eye for the truth, and having tasted it he now wants to abide in that supreme bliss. A devotee is one who is established at the heart; who, going beyond blind devotion, has reached the devotion of Experience of Being. His faith is at such a level, where the answers given to him, directly transport him to the Experience.

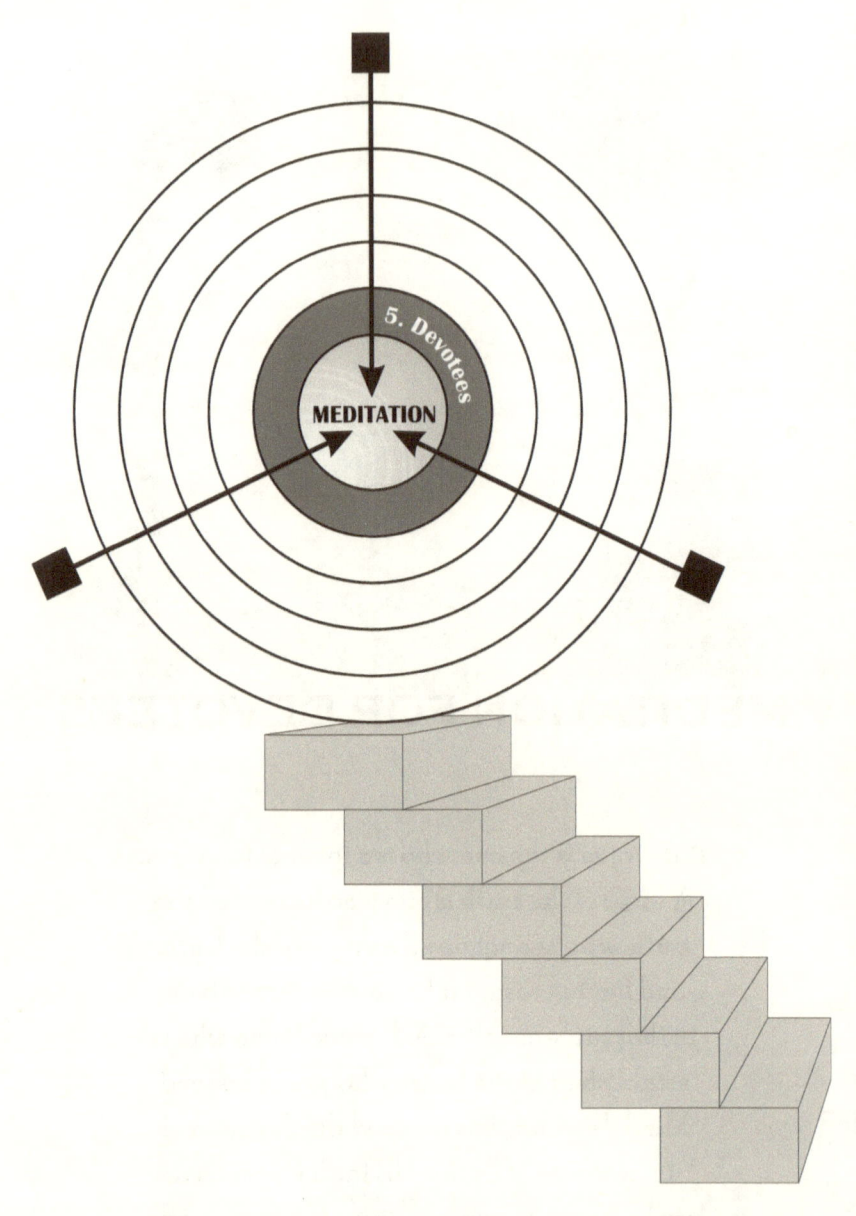

CHAPTER 15
Samadhi
UNDERSTANDING AND CONVICTION

When we focus our attention on something, it is 'concentration'. When we focus our attention on nothing, it is 'meditation.' To meditate on nothing is very difficult for the mind. Meditation on nothing leads to death of the mind. If the mind does not have the understanding of the truth, it will never get ready to die. Hence attain understanding before meditation. Just anyone cannot impart to you this understanding. For that you need a perceptor of time (one who knows the need of the time), who who will take you beyond time.

Q. 205 : What is Samadhi?

Sirshree : Samadhi is *samay* (time) *aadhi* (before); that which was before time. Samadhi means knowing and experiencing the entity that existed before the world was created. Time came later on. Time came only after the world was created. If in the waking state we reach the experience which is beyond time, beyond the body, mind and intellect, it has been called as samadhi. In this state the Creator of the universe is realised. And that Creator is within us. Spirituality is understanding the nature of His existence.

We reach the state of samadhi every night when we are in deep sleep. In that state, we simply do not realise how many hours have passed by. We realise this only when we wake up in the morning. The state which takes us beyond time is 'samadhi'. Every night we are in samadhi, but this samadhi is in unconsciousness. One can go into samadhi even in the conscious state.

Q. 206 : If we can go into samadhi in the waking state, then what is the obstacle?

Sirshree : Beliefs! Beliefs (false notions) have to be eliminated in order to go into samadhi. We have assumed some things to be true, but which are actually not true. If all our false beliefs are dispelled, samadhi is the only state that remains. You are looking for security outside. But the real security lies within you. When you realise your actual nature, then through that experience (samadhi), you will feel true security because you will realise that 'you are not the body.' Where is the body in sleep? Then how do you come to know that you had good sleep? This only means that there was someone who was awake, and that someone is you. The 'real you' was present who comes to know that you (body-mind) had good sleep. No matter how much suffering or pain you have, everything gets eliminated in the state of sleep.

Q. 207 : Then why don't we get convinced that we are not the body?

Sirshree : Every night in sleep the body disappears, but on waking in the morning we again slip into unconsciousness and again we start regarding ourselves to be the body. Due to association of the senses with the body, a world gets created – the world of vision through the eyes, the world of sound through the ears, the world of smell through the nose, the world of taste through the tongue and the world of touch through the skin. The experience of this world is so intense that we believe more in what is visible or felt through our senses.

Q. 208 : You told us what the goal is and also described samadhi. Then do you recommend that we go into samadhi or not?

Sirshree : Only those should go into samadhi who haven't yet attained the conviction and who are not yet ready to believe that they are beyond the body, mind and intellect.

We are talking about that thing which is present even now. It is going on right at this moment, but we are unable to grasp it. Understand this through an example:

A music is playing and we are sitting out here and conversing with each other. The music can be heard, but someone says, "I can't hear it." So, everyone is told, "Please maintain silence" and he will try to listen to the music.

When he is able to hear the music, he says to one person, "Okay, now you speak and I will see if I can still hear the music… Yes! I can still perceive it… Others can start speaking too." This signifies that he will now awaken every sense of his body and see if he is still able to perceive the music or not. In exactly the same manner, he has closed all his senses in samadhi and is listening to that entity (the Experience). Now he is strongly convinced that that entity is constantly going on. After this exercise, if he is able to perceive the Experience even after the awakening of all his senses, only then was going into samadhi fruitful for him.

THE BODY AND SAMADHI

Q. 209 : What is the relation between the body and samadhi?

Sirshree : Let us understand the relation between the body and samadhi with the help of an example.

Our body is a house of two rooms. There are different seasons surrounding this house. Sometimes it is rain, sometimes winter, sometimes summer and sometimes it is spring. Among the two rooms in the house, in the inner room there is a tube light which is always on. In the outer room, there is a tube light which goes off at times, there is a bulb which keeps going on and off (flickering) and there is a zero-bulb.

- In one season, all the lights are on. (The waking state)
- Another season arrives. The tube light in the inner room continues to glow. However, in the outer room, the tube light, the flickering bulb and the zero-bulb, all are off. (The state of sleep)
- A third season arrives in which the inner tube light is on as usual. In the outer room, the tube light is off. The flickering bulb is on. The zero-bulb is off too. (The dream state)
- In the fourth season, the outer tube light and the flickering bulb are off. But the zero-bulb is on. The inner tube light is on as always. (The state of samadhi)

✓ = on ✗ = off	Outer room of body		Inner room of body	
	Outer tube	Zero bulb	On-off bulb	Inner tube
1. Waking state	✓	✓	✓	✓
2. Sleeping state	✗	✗	✗	✓
3. Dream state	✗	✗	✓	✓
4. Samadhi (turiya) state	✗	✓	✗	✓

SUMMARY OF BODY STATES

In this way there are different seasons corresponding with different states of the body. We can understand this in the following manner:

    Outer tube   – Lots of thoughts

    Zero-bulb   – No thoughts/ thoughtlessness

    Flickering bulb   – Intermittent thoughts/ dream activity

    Inner tube   – Life, Experience of Being

1) **The waking state** – The tube light of both, the inner and outer rooms, are on. This signifies that there is awareness of our inner and outer consciousness. At this time the zero-bulb and the flickering bulb are on too. Man remains in this state for 16 hours.

2) **The sleep state** – When we are asleep, all the lights of the outer room are off. Only the inner tube light is on. We are in deep sleep. There are no dreams.

3) **The dream state** – Only the flickering bulb and the inner tube are on. The rest are all off. In this state, a person is dreaming. (The inner tube light is always on in all the four states as this

is the light that has been called Life or the Experience of Being).

4) **Samadhi** – The tube light in the inner room is on along with the outer zero-bulb. That means it is the thoughtless state, at the same time there is awareness of being thoughtless.

Q. 210 : How does meditation help in attaining samadhi?

Sirshree : Samadhi is the ultimate goal of meditation. Meditation will help you on the path of samadhi. Every session of meditation helps in your progress. It eliminates the beliefs, which act as obstacles between you and samadhi. Every time you practise the 'Who am I?' Meditation, you will receive a new direction. A new reality will dawn upon you. Each time, there will be a deeper attack on your wrong beliefs. Conviction will strengthen that you are not the body. The awareness of the experience of your being will awaken. Then you can directly go into samadhi.

SAHAJ (NATURAL) SAMADHI AND CONVICTION

Q. 211 : What are the types of samadhi?

Sirshree : Three types of samadhi have been described:

1) **Nirvikalpa Samadhi** – The state of samadhi which is entered without holding on to any support like breathing, mantra, etc.

2) **Savikalpa Samadhi** – The state of samadhi which is entered with the aid of techniques like concentrating on the breath, chanting a mantra, etc. Here effort is put in.

3) **Sahaj Samadhi** – You are naturally and effortlessly in the state of samadhi all the time, even while performing all your activities. Your goal is Sahaj Samadhi.

Q. 212 : What is the last state of meditation?

Sirshree : Samadhi is the last state of meditation. When you are in deep sleep, only the inner tube is on. All the external lights (activities) are absent. You want this state. When even the flickering bulb goes off, you say, "I had good sleep." Until now you have experienced three states – waking, dream, and sleep states. Now you have to know the fourth state. The fourth state is that where you reach the inner room in the waking state, which is known as samadhi. This state can be known only through experience.

Q. 213 : What will be the most significant thing at the *tejasthan* (bright place)?

Sirshree : Nothing. *Tejasthan* stands for that place which is outside of inside and outside. This cannot be understood in the language of the mind. When we say 'nothing', it literally means 'nothing' in the language of the mind. But in the *tej* (Bright) language or language of wisdom, nothing does not mean nothing. It is Bright Nothing. When the mind enters into nothing, it then becomes 'no-mind' (where the mind does not exist) or it bows down and surrenders to the Self.

What is there at the *tejasthan* cannot be described. But what is not there can be described. There the mind, ego, time, colour, form, age, space, and the world do not exist.

Q. 214 : What is the understanding that one has to attain?

Sirshree : The understanding of 'Who am I?' Otherwise people have mistaken sitting with eyes closed for hours together as samadhi. Through this the mind only grows stronger instead of being eliminated. It feels 'I went into samadhi.' Hence in *tejgyan* (Bright or Supreme Knowledge), importance has been given to understanding. Samadhi can be attained through understanding alone. And only in samadhi can you attain 100% conviction of your true nature. It is then that the death of the individual 'I' occurs and the Bright 'I' (Universal 'I') awakens. The ultimate aim of samadhi is the conviction that, 'I am not the body.' This is similar to the conviction a girl has that she is a girl. She does not need to repeatedly remind herself that she is a girl. Every moment, while sitting, standing, walking, eating and in every activity, she has the feeling of being a girl. In samadhi, this is the kind of conviction that you need to attain about 'who you are'. If this does not happen and your conviction does not grow, then samadhi is useless for you.

Q. 215 : How can conviction be attained?

Sirshree : By attaining the final knowledge through listening. Final knowledge means 'Bright knowledge'. Bright knowledge signifies knowledge that is beyond knowledge and ignorance. Here the seeker is told the final truth, the supreme truth. The beginning itself is made with the end. Hence it has been called as the final knowledge. Beginning with the end implies that the missing link is made clear. The seeker attains final understanding here, where the see-er is seen and the knower is known. Where the realisation is attained that you don't have to do 'meditation', but you are meditation. Meditation only needs to be understood. You don't have to do anything. The music (bliss) within you is constantly going on. But to be able to listen to it, the external noise needs to stop. Final Knowledge is the preparation to stop that noise.

Q. 216 : My mind does not go within.

Sirshree : The mind does not go within because what is within is unknown to it. Everyone knows what is outside. We go to our home; we go to our office, everything is familiar. We go to all places familiar to us but not to unknown places. Hence first get acqainted with the unknown. Find out what lies within. The more you listen to the truth and attend the Final Truth discourses, the more internal things will be talked about, things related to the *tejasthan* will be talked about. Thereby you will get the inspiration to go within and feel enthusiastic to enter the state of *moun* (Silence). Now it is only the beginning. Further on you will be so eager to take a dip within that you will think, "When will I go into *moun*...? When will I get the time...? When will I go within?" This will happen spontaneously. Till such a state arrives, tell your mind that the inside is unknown and outside we know everything, hence it is feeling the resistance.

Related to this is another question that the mind sometimes is able to go within and sometimes it is not. The answer to this is: 'The mind when turned inside is like a monk. But when turned outside, it is like a monkey.' It is good that your mind at least goes inside sometimes, there are many whose minds never turn inwards. Very soon this 'sometimes' will become 'just now' for you. Which means that when someone asks you, "Did you go within?" You will reply, "I am just coming from there." If someone asks you, "Have you been to the temple?" You will tell him, "Yes! I am just coming from there." As you wake up from sleep, if someone asks you, "Did you go to the temple?" You will say the same thing, "I am just returning from there." This implies that the mind is frequently going within. And if this happens repeatedly then 'sometimes' will very soon become 'just now'. Consequently the mind that was able to go within sometimes, will now be going within all the time.

Q. 217 : Can the Experience of Being be outside the body as well?

Sirshree : What you want to ask is – does the *tejasthan* exist outside the body as well? Let us understand the answer to this question through different examples:

1) "Does the *rasgulla* (an Indian dish consisting of a sweet ball soaked in sugar syrup) have syrup inside it or outside it?" You would say, "The *rasgulla* is permeated by the syrup, it has syrup inside it as well as outside it." Likewise the Experience exists within as well as without.

2) A fish lives in water. There is water all around it and it lives inside that very water. The existence of the fish is in the water. But it may go about searching for water, thinking where does the water exist… This is because the water is so close to it and touching its eyes that it does not realise that it is *in* the water. The Experience too is so close to us that we don't realise whether we exist in that experience or the experience is within us. The fact is that the *tejasthan* surrounds us from all sides. The body is present in the experience just like the fish in water.

3) When you fry a *bhajji* (an Indian deep-fried dish) in oil, there is oil within it as well as outside of it. Likewise, the experience is within the body as well as outside all around it.

NOTE:

Those whose aim is to attain the ultimate truth need to know that any technique may be helpful for them to attain the truth, but they should not take the technique itself to be the ultimate truth.

Here it is important to understand that there is no connection between the techniques and the truth. But yes, you will derive happiness from both. By practising the techniques, the happiness you will attain is the same that you get by going to a carnival, which has been called as temporary happiness, that lasts only for a few moments. Then there is the happiness that is attained through listening to the truth, which has been called as permanent happiness. It is present every moment, constant in every incident, it is within you and never changes. For this you will have to listen to the Bright Truth. There may be a question in the minds of people as to how can liberation be attained only through listening? How can Self Realisation be attained? The answer to this question is – through listening, you gain understanding. As soon as you gain understanding, actions take place automatically. Actually, listening, understanding and action are not three. They are one.

For example, a snake appeared on your path. You mistook it to be a rope. At that moment if someone warns you that it is not a rope but a snake, your listening, understanding and action will all occur at the same time. You will take evasive action at once. Hence you only have to listen – listen to the truth and not about the truth. Listening to the truth and listening about the truth are two different things. You have to listen to the pure truth, which is imparted through Bright knowledge or *tejgyan*. There are many who are very close to the truth. They are sitting on the dynamite of truth. A little spark, a small indication, listening to which the dynamite of truth will explode and the seeker will attain Self Realisation. For these people, just listening is enough.

Listening was the very first path. In the ancient times, the sages imparted knowledge to their disciples according to their Gita. If a disciple did not understand through listening, only then he was given some technique to practise. In Tej Gyan Foundation too, people are given guidance according to their Gita, which helps them attain the truth in the most simple and speedy manner.

Neither is silence meditation,
nor do we need to meditate on sounds.
We don't have to do meditation.
Bright Silence in itself is meditation.

CHAPTER 16

Who Am I

'WHO AM I' MEDITATION

On continuously watching thoughts, you notice their crowd diminishing. You will begin to observe the gap between thoughts. This observation will enhance your understanding of meditation and will give you the key to Self Meditation.

Q. 218 : Who am I?

Sirshree : Before seeking the answer to "Who am I?", ask yourself, "Who I am not?"

- I am not this body because, when I say that this is my body, then it becomes mine and not 'me.'
- I am not 'my car' because I drive the car.
- 'My house' cannot possibly be me because I say, "Come to my house," and not "Come into me."
- The name given to this body is not me because it was given to me after I was born.
- The five elements of this physical body – ether, air, fire, water and earth, are not me.
- The astral body within this physical body is not me.
- The five senses of the body – eyes, ears, nose, tongue and skin, are not me. I use these senses.
- I am not those things that are related to the senses – sight, sound, smell, taste and touch.
- I am also not the breath, due to which this body-mind mechanism functions.
- Neither am I the mind that thinks about what I should be.
- Nor am I the intellect that is absent along with the body during deep sleep.

Q. 219 : If I am not all these, then what is it that remains that I can be?

Sirshree : You alone are the one who remains.

- You alone are the one who is using the five bodies. You alone are the master of the intellect. You alone are the witness of the mind.
- Now you are beyond every label.
- If you no longer are the body, the mind and the intellect, then how can you be an engineer or a doctor or a leader or a student?
- How can you be a brother, sister, father, mother, friend, husband, wife, disciple or Guru?
- How can you be black, white, short, tall or fat?
- How can you be an Indian, American, British or Chinese?
- How can you be a Hindu, Muslim, Christian or a Jew?
- How can you be cheerful, intelligent, foolish, positive, active, lazy, honest or benevolent?
- Now it is just you who remains – pure, without any name or form.

Accept your true form as it is and abide in it. You have become something that you are not. Now is the time to be established in your consciousness; to be who you really are – the Bright Witness, the Bright 'I', the Universal 'I'.

Q. 220 : How should we do the 'Who am I' Meditation?

Sirshree : People usually meditate by uttering a word such as 'Om' or repeating some mantra or aphorism from the sacred texts.

But, these are not as effective to enhance your awareness about yourself as the question, 'Who am I?' Many who meditate do not know whether they are meditating or sleeping or are merely in a hazy state of mind. You cannot go to sleep or be in a hazy state when you ask the question, "Who am I?" You become alert for the answer immediately after asking the question. This question pierces within like a spear and drives you in straight to your centre. In the beginning you may not be able to recognise the deep silence or *moun* even on reaching your centre. However, by continuously persisting with this question, you will gradually begin to recognise the Bright Silence or *tejasthan* within. Then this question itself will begin to become the answer.

However advanced a meditator is, thoughts keep crowding in his mind. We need a very potent thought to annihilate these thoughts. Just as you require steel to cut through steel, poison to antidote the effects of poison, you require a thought to annihilate all other thoughts. "Who am I?" is such a thought that will end every thought, false belief, concept and imaginary idea. All that is needed is to learn the art of using this weapon.

Whenever a thought appears – be it of fear, greed, hatred, repulsion or worry, just ask yourself, "To whom has this thought occurred?" or, "Who is afraid?" or, "Who is feeling the hatred?" Then the answer will come as, "I." Now ask, "Who is this I?" No sooner this question arises than you will reach your centre and for some time you will be immersed in the silence or moun within. It is in this silence that the light of the truth (supreme knowledge) emerges. After a few moments another thought will appear. You will again ask the question as to whom has this thought occurred. The answer will come as, "To me." Again ask, "Who am I?"

You may begin this enquiry for 20 minutes a day, and very soon you will be able to carry out this enquiry all day long along with your daily activities. You will begin to know the answer at the experiential level. You will begin to experience the answer. Finally a stage will arrive where all the thoughts will be annihilated and then the last thought – "Who am I?" will also end. All that will remain is realisation of the Self, experience of the Unlimited, 'Bright Knowlerience' (ultimate knowledge arising out of Experience). (To understand this meditation more in detail, read the book 'Self Enquiry with Understanding').

Continue this enquiry until you recognise your true identity; until all imaginary concepts about yourself do not completely dissolve – such as the concept that you are the body. Once all the beliefs dissolve, Self-enquiry will end on its own as you will then be stabilised on your Self. After that, even if there are thoughts, you would have understood that these are not my thoughts, they do not occur to me; I am the Bright Witness beyond them. Thoughts are in my body-mind mechanism. This mechanism is only a mirror that makes me aware of myself. 'If thoughts are going on in this mirror, then how does it trouble me?! The mirror is doing its job of making me experience my Self or Being.' Practising Self-enquiry and being established on oneself is the greatest devotion. Eliminating thoughts the moment they arise by the process of Self-enquiry is the truest sacrifice or renunciation of all.

Q. 221 : What are the points to be taken care of in this meditation?

Sirshree : After asking the question "Who am I?", the meditator begins to give answers through the intellect saying, "I am this" or, "I am not this." But the technique suggests that you do not have to give answers in words, but reach the source of thoughts; reach that Experience, even if it is only for a few moments. Through constant practice, you will begin to remain on the Self and the mind will want to go to its source. The Experience from within is important and not the answers of the intellect. You need to go to that place from where the thoughts originate (Bright place – *tejasthan*).

- The mind seeks quick results. "What was the benefit of my performing Self-enquiry today?" The mind wishes to assess. Impatience is just another aspect of the mind. Enquire, "Who is impatient?"

- Some people might think that this is a technique to suppress thoughts or to develop concentration. No. This technique is only meant to awaken your source. Concentration increases on its own. Thoughts are not suppressed, but they dissolve in the inner silence (moun). This is where you attain true happiness or unremitting bliss.

- Some might think that we should think in detail about all the thoughts that are arising within us and only then ask ourself, "Whom have these thoughts occurred to?" It is not so. The moment you become aware of a thought arising, cut it in between and ask, "Whom is this thought occurring to? If it is occurring to me, then who am I?" Then stay in the 'feeling of being.' After some practice this will begin to become easy and spontaneous.

- You might wonder as to what is the relation between Self-enquiry and peace. But absolute silence is your nature. You do not have to become silence but just realise that you are silence, you are awareness (Bright awareness), Bright Witness. Attachment to thoughts alone has put us into unhappiness. Through continuous enquiry when you begin to be on your true self, you will experience supreme peace.

- During the process of Self enquiry, you could come across many experiences such as seeing a light, disappearing of the feeling of the body, hearing some kind of sounds or music, etc. But at such a time you have to enquire, "Who is it that is seeing the light?" "Who is it that is hearing the sounds?" and reach your source every time.

- You don't have to fight with the mind. Actually, it is the mind that wants to fight with the mind. Instead of fighting, you have to just know where these thoughts are emerging from and go to their source.

- In the beginning you will be able to remain on your true self for small periods of time. But with time and constant practice, being on yourself will become natural and spontaneous. This is what has been called as Sahaj or Natural Samadhi.

- One may commit the mistake of repeating continuously, "Who am I...? Who am I...?" without ever being on the 'I' experience. Such a person is only chanting the question like a mantra. This will fetch him the benefits of chanting a mantra, but he will never realise the answer to "Who am I?" Even on asking, "Who am I?" just once, if you reach the feeling of your being (Self), it is enough. After asking "Who am I?", concentrate your entire attention on the feeling of "I am."

Q. 222 : What should I actually do during meditation?

Sirshree : Do not think anything and also do not think as to how you should not think of anything. To attain this state, various meditation techniques have been explained in the next chapter. With regular practice of these techniques, you can attain the state of Samadhi.

Meditation is that art where one learns the technique of surrendering the mind (ego).

Through this technique, surrending does not give you slavery, instead it sets you free.

When one begins to remember the Self,
meditation then becomes Supreme Knowledge.

CHAPTER 17

The Method And Techniques of Meditation

Seven MEDITATION TECHNIQUES

Some people went to meet a Guru in a hermitage, but they were stopped at the gate. There were some balls lying outside the gate. They were told, "You can play with these balls in the meantime. There is a target over there, you can aim for it. Just do something for passing time." They kept on playing but how long could they play? At last they got fed up. Some people decided to leave. However, some people waited and continued to play. While playing this game, suddenly one person went inside the hermitage. The remaining people did not understand why he went in.

Later, when this man who had gone inside met the remaining people, everybody asked him, "Why did you go inside?" He replied, "All of you were playing with the balls, but did you read what was written on those balls? There were different words written on each ball. But they all added up to mean: If you get tired of playing, come inside."

This means that even though these people were playing with the balls, their attention was not on the balls. Even when accidentally their attention went on a ball, because of reading just one word disconnectedly they could not understand its meaning. But when this man noticed a word, a question appeared in his mind, "What is this word?" He examined all the words written on each ball and arrived at the final message by decoding each of them. He then went inside the hermitage. He got the understanding that going inside (to go inside the hermitage, which also signifies going within ourself) is very easy and simple.

If today somebody is asked to go within, they would say, "We do go within but we don't find anything. You say that there is something, but when we go there, there is nothing." Thoughts are continuously going on in their minds but they are not able to grasp that the one who is seeing these thoughts and knowing them (the witness) is there too. It is due to the lack of this understanding that they immediately come out from within.

From this story what we have to understand is that the game is going on, i.e. the activities of our physical world are constantly going on, but when somebody gets tired of it, he then should go within (at the heart, tejasthan). However, some get tired of the game, yet they do not go within, rather they go out because this game is being played without any awareness. If the game is going on without awareness, then nothing will happen. Whatever you do, do it with awareness. Learn to focus your attention through practice.

You have understood that there are various stages of meditation.

These are:

- Prayer
- Relaxation
- Contemplation
- Concentration
- Willpower
- Self-observation with Awareness

There are various meditation techniques at each of these levels. In the following pages, one or two meditation techniques have been described for each of these levels. The focus of this book is Complete Meditation. Complete Meditation is when Self Observation with Awareness occurs. The final meditation mentioned in this book – Complete Meditation – is the most important of all. Before understanding Complete Meditation, understand one meditation at each level and then we shall bring together all to practise Complete Meditation; to attain self observation with awareness. Then meditation shall be complete.

1. **INTENTION MEDITATION (LEVEL : PRAYER)**

You perform 'intention meditation' before you begin any meditation. Close your eyes and pray from the bottom of your heart that you shall get the best results of meditation. This is the first prayer. In this prayer, you keep a strong intention that you shall be undisturbed and be fully benefited by meditation. Along with this, remind yourself that you do not have any expectation that a particular experience should occur. This is the second prayer. In this prayer, tell God or the Higher Source that you are open to whatever experiences that may occur in meditation and you leave it to Him to manifest what He wants. Thus the second prayer is to ask God for manifesting in meditation what He wants rather than what you want. The words for these two prayers can be your own. But essentially these two seemingly paradoxical prayers mean that you have a strong intention for best results, but have no expectation for a particular experience. The summary of this meditation can be said in the following words, "My will is that I should be benefited. But, thy will is my will."

2. RELAX BUTTON MEDITATION (LEVEL : RELAXATION)

Let us understand this meditation. If you have programmed yourself that whenever you join your thumb and index finger () of one hand, you will go into a relaxed state or in a state of meditation, then you can adopt this mudra () whenever you are under stress and get stress-free instantly. If your body gets habituated to your sitting in meditation with the thumb and index finger joined together, then this signal will have an instant effect on your body. If you want to go into a particular emotional state, then on joining your thumb and index finger together, you will automatically experience that state. For example, when you go to a temple (or mosque or church) and join your hands together, then what kind of feeling do you get? Right now, check your feeling. Now join your hands together and bow your head a bit just like you do in a temple. Now check the feeling within you. You will notice that your feeling has changed. You will experience the same feeling that you do in a temple. Your mind has identified this gesture. Now whenever this gesture is repeated, the mind goes into the feeling of being in a temple. That means 'folding your hands' has become a signal for your body. Whenever you fold your hands, your body gets a signal that it should go into the feeling of being in a temple. In the same way, when you will join your thumb and index finger, your body will get the indication and you will become mentally prepared to go into the state that you have programmed it for.

Benefits :

1. When you are on stage and if you are feeling tensed, then joining your thumb and index finger at that time will relax you instantly.

2. You can utilise this relax button while walking, sitting, standing, in your shop, in court, in office or wherever you work. When you join your thumb and index finger, it means you are using a 'relax button' or 'press button' because whenever you have been relaxed or entered meditation, you have joined your thumb and index finger, due to which your body has developed this signal. As soon as your body gets this signal, it starts working in that direction. On joining your thumb and index finger together, you can bring forth the same feeling of relaxation. Once your body develops this programming, then you can benefit from it all your life.

3. When a student is studying, he should do so with the thumb and index finger of one hand joined together. Then if he cannot remember something during his examination, he can join his thumb and index finger. This will bring back the state of mind he had during his study and he will start remembering the answers.

In this way, you can prepare a 'press button'. Whenever one prays, one does so with hands joined together. Prayer can be done without joining the hands, but whosoever made these rules, did so after much thinking and understanding. It is not necessary that you should make a press button only with your thumb and index finger. In order to programme yourself, you can use any press button, touching which you instantly get the same state of mind for which you have programmed yourself; and you should use it only for that purpose. This is very beneficial. An even bigger advantage is that as soon as you touch the press button, you will be transported to that state instantly; this can happen within a second. That is why whenever you practise any meditation, prior to that habituate yourself to meditating with your thumb and finger joined together.

3. WISDOM MEDITATION (LEVEL : CONTEMPLATION)

You can try the following experiment right now as soon as you have finished reading this part. What you need to understand before the experiment is: You are using your body; you are not the body. You use a car, but you never say, "I am this car." You always say, "This is my car." With whatever word you use 'my', you cannot be that (my house, my eyes, etc.). To understand this in depth, try the experiment given below.

Look at one of your hands and ask yourself, "Am I this hand?" Answer this question with your feeling and not with your intellect. Give yourself a minute to feel it. Again, look at your hand and ask yourself, "Am I this hand?" What relation do you feel with your hand?... Am I this hand?... Look at it carefully.

The experience or feeling you get is: 'It is my hand, but I am not this hand.' In the same way, repeat the same thing with every part of your body (feet, knees, face, etc.). Then what feeling do you get... 'I am not this.'

The next question you should ask yourself is, "If this hand is cut, then do I become incomplete?" "No, I am still complete." The feeling, the experience that is present within says, "I am complete."

A person's hands and legs may be amputated due to an accident, but still he says, "I am there." He never says, "I am incomplete... earlier I was complete, now I am incomplete." Because when the body is cut, you (the real you) do not get cut. When you begin to experience this truth, then the root belief that 'I am this body' will break.

Thus in this meditation, contemplate on 'Who am I?' through the body.

4. Sound Meditation (Level : Concentration)

1. Close your eyes and sit in the meditation posture with a proper mudra.
2. Keeping the body steady, listen to all the sounds around you and try to detect and identify five different types of sounds.
3. If there is the sound of a rotating fan, then there could be various other sounds contained in that sound, listen to them carefully. Various types of sounds can include conversations of people, clattering of vessels, children playing, horns and sounds of different vehicles. There can be the sound of something falling, the sound of somebody's footsteps, the sounds of television, radio or music system, the sound of birds chirping, the sound of dogs barking or fighting. There can also be the sounds of water flowing, the sound of a whistle or the sound of somebody laughing or crying. When there are no sounds, then try to perceive the sound of silence. Feel the stillness.
4. Try to detect every type of sound around you. If you can hear the sound of an aeroplane flying, then there are different sounds of different types of aeroplanes. Try to identify even the minutest of sounds. After identifying five different types of sounds, slowly open your eyes.
5. Every week, go on increasing the number of sounds.

5. Breathing Meditation (Level : Concentration)

1. Sit in an appropriate posture and mudra of meditation.
2. Relax yourself by taking one or two deep breaths and then releasing slowly.
3. Subsequently let your breathing continue to be as it is at present – shallow breathing or deep breathing, comfortable,

natural... however it may be, let it continue the same. If you control your breathing, then it is not meditation; it is pranayam (breath regulation).

4. Be aware whether the breath is going in or coming out... now it went in... now it came out... from the right nostril... from the left nostril... or from both nostrils. Be aware of every direction and every state (cold or warm) of the breath.

5. Focus your mind on the breath that is going in and coming out. Perceive the breath that is going in and identify the breath that is coming out... it went in... it came out... went in... came out. Just remain aware of your breathing as it is – natural breathing, comfortable and easy breathing.

6. Sometimes your breathing will be deep, sometimes shallow. Keeping the body steady, remain aware of the coming and going of every breath.

7. Practise this meditation for 20-45 minutes as per your convenience. After some time when you become an expert in this meditation, then meditate on the interval between two breaths.

6. THOUGHTS MEDITATION (LEVEL : WILLPOWER)

1. Close your eyes and sit in the meditation posture.

2. Begin to watch your thoughts. See which thoughts are going on inside you.

3. Keeping the body steady, continue watching the types of thoughts that are going on in your mind from a distance (i.e. without getting identified; remaining separate or detached). Use all your willpower to not move the body and not to pursue any thought. In this meditation, by being separate, you will know what kind of thoughts go on in your mind about various subjects.

4. Continue watching and knowing your thoughts like a witness. Do not label any thought as 'good' or 'bad'. Avoid any desires such as, 'I want more thoughts' or 'I don't want any thoughts.'

5. Initially practise this meditation for five minutes and gradually go on increasing the time. When you become an expert in this meditation, then start giving numbers to your thoughts.

7. COMPLETE MEDITATION (LEVEL: SELF OBSERVATION WITH AWARENESS)

In all the above meditations, experiencing the experiencer was missing. Thus they were incomplete. Meditation is complete only when self observation with awareness occurs. Complete Meditation brings together all the six individual meditations seen so far and then at the end of the last three meditations seen above, asks you to turn within to see who is doing the meditation. When you turn within to ask who is meditating, the mind falls. The mind becomes the boss when Consciousness goes to sleep. The mind becomes a servant when Consciousness, backed by the strength of Complete Meditation, announces itself as the boss. What happens in Complete Meditation? The Experiencer experiences the Experiencer in the Experience.

Begin this meditation by following the procedure given below. First read this procedure again and again and imbibe it fully well in your mind. You can also record all the instructions sequentially on a tape and then playing the tape you can begin the meditation according to the instructions being given.

1. Close your eyes and pray for best results with no expectation that something particular should happen. Then, sit in a meditation posture (*sukhasan* or any convenient posture) with a *mudra (dhyan mudra* or any other preferred mudra).

2. Keeping the body steady, listen to all the sounds around you. Identify at least five different sounds. Do not be in hurry.

With a quiet mind, focus your attention on various sounds. Don't get stuck with a particular sound and start listening only to that. Just identify the sound and move ahead.

3. If there is the sound of the rotating fan, then there are other subtle sounds within that sound too. Listen to them attentively. Various types of sounds can include conversations of people, clattering of vessels, children playing, horns and sounds of different vehicles. There can be the sound of something falling, the sound of somebody's footsteps, the sounds of television, music system or radio, the sound of birds, the sound of dogs barking or fighting. There can also be the sounds of water flowing, the sound of a whistle or the sound of somebody laughing or crying. When there are no sounds, then try to perceive the sound of silence. Feel the stillness.

4. Try to detect every type of sound around you. If you can hear the sound of an aeroplane in the sky, then there are different sounds of different types of aeroplanes. Try to identify even the minutest of sounds. Listen to at least five different sounds – loud, medium or subtle.

5. After having listened to different sounds, ask yourself, "Am I these sounds?" The reply will come from within you, "I am not these sounds, I am the one who is knowing these sounds." Then turn within and see who this knower is, who is the ear of the ear. Tell yourself, "I am not the sound."

6. Now concentrate your attention on the atmosphere. Feel the atmosphere all around you and see whether it is hot or cold or dry or humid, whether the body feels light or heavy, whether there is a swift breeze or a gentle wind or fresh air or less air.

7. If you are able to feel the air, the heat or cold, then ask yourself, "Am I this atmosphere?" A reply will emerge, "No,

I am not this atmosphere. I am the one who is perceiving or knowing this atmosphere." Then tell yourself, "Turn around", and know the one who is knowing. Tell yourself, "I am not this atmosphere."

8. Now concentrate your attention on your body. If there is stiffness or pain in any part of the body, just know it experientially. Do not let the body move even a bit.

9. In the whole body, where lightness or heaviness is felt, where clothes are touching, the air is touching, where itching or dryness is felt, where there is sweating, where there is a burning sensation – feel those parts. This way, see all the subtle or gross sensations inside and outside the body.

10. Here 'seeing' means 'knowing'. Do not imagine anything; just feel what is happening in or on the body. Do not drive away the feeling of what is happening at present. Do not consider that feeling as good or bad; just feel it as it is. After seeing all the sensations, after knowing what is happening in the whole body, ask yourself, "Am I these sensations?" The reply that will arise will be, "No, I am not these sensations. I am the knower of these sensations." Then immediately turn around and shift to the knower, reach there. Tell yourself, "I am not these sensations."

11. Now focus your attention on your breathing. Just watch how the breathing is going on. Feel through which nostril you are inhaling and through which nostril you are exhaling. When the breath is going inside, you are aware of the breath going inside. When the breath is coming out, then too you are aware that the breath is coming out.

12. When the breath goes through your nose and dashes against the opening of the nostril, you are able to feel the contact of the breath. Whether the air that goes in and that which comes out is warm or not, know this as deeply as possible.

13. If your attention goes astray in between, then bring it back on your breathing again. Whether the breath went inside silently or with a sound, came out silently or with a sound – perceive this too. Whether the breath is shallow, deep or heavy, however be the breath, keep knowing it without labelling it.

14. Whether the breath is coming out through the left nostril or the right, continue to observe this. In this way you are preparing for meditation and going towards Self Meditation (meditation on the Self). Ask yourself, "Am I this breath?" The reply will emerge, "No, I am not this breath. I am the knower of the breath." Now know this knower and tell yourself, "I am not the breath."

15. Now shift your attention from breathing and focus it on the thoughts that arise within. Watch the thoughts that are arising in your mind at this moment. After knowing one thought, know the next thought that arises. There is no need to pursue the previous thought. Just watch a thought and say, "Next." If you get a thought such as, 'There are no thoughts arising at all', then you have to understand that this is also a thought. After seeing it, say, "Next." As you go on watching thoughts, you will also feel the joy of detachment from thoughts. Watching all the thoughts that are arising in the mind, ask yourself, "Am I these thoughts?" The reply will come, "No, I am not the thoughts, I am the knower of thoughts." Now know that knower. Without moving the body, know the thoughts, and tell yourself, "I am not these thoughts."

16. Now focus your attention on your hands. Know as to how you are feeling in the hands. Now take your attention to your arms and experience how you are feeling there. See whether you are able to feel the arms or not or whether they feel heavy or light. Just know whatever you are feeling. Ask yourself, "Am I these hands?" The reply will appear, "No, I am not these

hands, I am knowing these hands." Immediately turn back your attention within and know the one who is knowing these hands. Even if you are unable to know the knower (your true self), continue the meditation without getting disappointed.

17. Now take your attention to both your legs. If you are not the hands, then who are you? To know this, take your attention to your legs. See whether you are able to feel your legs or not, whether there is pressure on them or lightness is felt in them. Without putting a label of good or bad, ask yourself, "Am I these legs?" The answer will appear, "No, I am the knower of these legs." Then know that knower. Tell yourself, "I am not the legs." If you are not the legs, then who are you? Ask yourself this question.

18. To find this answer, take your attention to the back. See how your back feels. Just know how it is feeling from the shoulders to the waist, whether it is feeling light, heavy, painful or if there is any pressure. Ask yourself, "Am I this back?" The reply will come, "No, I am the knower of this back." Shifting your focus within, know that knower, and tell yourself, "I am not this back."

19. Now bring your attention to your torso and the heart. Continue to perceive how the whole region feels. Ask yourself, "Am I the abdomen, am I the stomach or kidneys, am I the heart, am I the neck, am I the shoulders? If I am not all these, then who am I? I am the knower of all these parts." Immediately shift your attention and know that knower.

20. Now focus your attention on your face. If you are not the torso, then feel your face. See whether you are able to feel your face or not, whether you feel lightness on the face or some sweat on the face. Whether you feel pressure on the eyes or do the eyes feel light, know this. Then ask yourself, "Am I this

face?" The reply will emerge, "No, I am the knower of this face." Shifting your focus, know that knower.

21. Tell yourself, "I am not this face, I am not this body, I am not the parts of this body, I am not the breath that is going on in this body, I am not the thoughts, I am not the mind which is nothing but a bundle of thoughts; then who am I? I am the knower of these. I have associated with this body to meditate on the Self and to know the Self." As soon as you get this understanding, your attachment to the body will break. You will use your body, not vice versa. After some time, while remaining in this state open your eyes.

22. After opening your eyes, while still being in the same experience, go outside for a walk. Watch your body walking or working.

Contemplate on the understanding that you achieved, the freshness and the internal energy you attained and the shifting you received from this experience. Contemplate also on what you learnt and understood from the Complete Meditation. This understanding, this awareness will transform you and stabilise you on Self Realisation.

Complete Meditation is essential for every person just like taking a bath every day. By practising this meditation daily, our mind's slate will be become clean every day. By filling the mind with thoughts and due to not cleaning the slate, stress is built up. This meditation liberates you from stress and provides you the bliss of Self Realisation.

BRIGHT SILENCE ROOM
(Tej Moun Kaksha)
Good Mouning Room
(silence or *moun* + ing = Good Mouning)

Because of the constant somersault of thoughts, there is a constant load on the mind. When thoughts reduce, the body experiences deep peace. This peace can be achieved very simply and easily with meditation.

Meditation is a type of energy. On whatever we meditate, that thing starts coming towards us. Then whether we meditate with awareness or without awareness, that thing begins to move towards us. To give direction to this energy with awareness, meditation rooms have been created.

There are many factors that help in meditation, the most important among which is 'place.' If the place is right, then you can meditate more easily.

Hence, it helps to create a particular room, or a space in your house exclusively for your practice of meditation. This helps the mind attune to the state of meditation quicker when you are seated at this exclusive place. You can call it the "Bright Silence Room".

Glossary

Word	Meaning
Tej	*Tej* is one of the most important words coined by Sirshree. 'Bright' is the closest translation of this word. Let us understand Bright or *Tej* with the help of an example. There is happiness and there is unhappiness. Here happiness means opposite of unhappiness. But there also exists happiness that is beyond both these polarities. That is called *Tej* Happiness or Bright Happiness. This means that when the word '*Tej*' or 'Bright' is used as an adjective, then the word that is described as 'Bright' is beyond both polarities or beyond duality.
Tejguru	Spiritual master who guides you towards attainment of the supreme truth and stabilisation in that truth.
Tej/Bright Truth	The Supreme Truth which is beyond truth and lies, it is the ultimate reality.
Tej Parkhi	Bright Perceptor – the one who imparts to you the discerning eye for the Truth which is beyond duality. It means the one who recognises what is the need of the times and teaches the Truth accordingly. Tej Parkhi is not a name but the work (just like a doctor or an engineer). It is a state just as the name 'Buddha' is also a state.
Tejgyan	Bright Knowledge – knowledge of the supreme truth which is beyond duality, beyond the grasp of the senses. If the knowledge is at the level of the body it means knowledge through the senses of hearing, seeing, touch and feeling. But that which is beyond duality, beyond the intellect, mind and body is tejgyan.

Tej *Moun*	Tej *Moun* signifies the state of inner silence which is the intrinsic nature of our true self. It is the state beyond sound and silence, beyond speech and thought. Words appear from this inner silence and also disappear in it. There is silence between every word and behind every word. There is silence between every thought and behind every thought. On the paper of silence, the words of thought are written. To attain this silence is to attain Self.
Tejasthan	*Tejasthan* literally means the Bright Place. *Tejasthan* actually means that place where the Self is connected with our body; where the formless and the form unite, where the union (yog) takes place. It can be roughly considered to be in the area of the heart. At some places in the book, it has been loosely translated as the 'heart'. The second or external meaning of Tejasthan is a place where the knowledge of the truth is imparted.
Sadhak	A seeker whose quest has come into action, who has begun to practise.
Sadhana	The practice specified by the guru to a disciple which is meant for his spiritual progress.
Self	The Universal Self, our true self, our original nature, Consciousness, Life, the Formless, the Self-Witness, the Creator, God, Lord, Shiva, Allah…
Self Realisation	Realising who you are; realising your true essence or your original nature.
Self Stabilisation	Stabilising in the experience of Self Realisation or constantly being in the Experience of the Self (or Experience of Being) This is what can be termed as the final liberation or *moksh*.
Samadhi	The state of consciousness before time began. *Samadhi* is a state which cannot be adequately

described in words; it can only be experienced. It can be said that *Samadhi* is being conscious of the true self, transcending time and space. Or being in the state of undifferentiated beingness; a state of complete calm, tranquility and joy but where the mind continues to be alert. A second meaning is voluntarily entering the state of death, conscious death, arranged death, which is possible only with highly advanced saints and yogis.

Contrast Mind — 'Contrast mind' is a term used to distinguish between the two distinctive types of functioning of the mind. First is the intuitive mind, which is essential for our functioning. Second is the contrast mind which signifies that mind which compares and judges everything. It splits everything into two – white or black (good or bad), like the contrast control feature of the television. This is the mind which gives rise to fear, worry, envy, insecurity, deceit, assumptions, anger... In fact, it is the root cause of all the miseries in human life. It is only present in humans. It is that entity which blocks us from seeing the supreme truth.

BMM — Body-mind mechanism of man.

Maya — This whole world is *Maya*. *Maya* is generally regarded as illusion. However, there is a subtle distinction regarding the nature of *maya* versus illusion. Illusion is generally used to refer to something that does not exist. Maya, on the other hand, is existent and non-existent at the same time, like a dream. The experience you have seems to be absolutely real while the dream is occurring; therefore, the *maya* of this dream cannot be called non-existent. Yet, through the sobriety of wakefulness, one can see that the dream was an illusion, a false world.

Discourse	A speech that transcends words and takes you beyond the mind. Through discourses, knowledge of the truth is imparted.
Devotion	Intense feeling of a mixture of love and veneration for God.
Gita	It is an important religious text which contains the knowledge and guidance provided by Lord Krishna to Arjuna. In Tej Gyan Foundation it is said that the since the body-mind makeup of each individual is different, hence the 'Gita' of each is different. This means that the tendencies and state of every person is different and hence the guidance for each is different.
Individual	The entity within us which thinks itself to be separate from others.
Viveka	The power of discrimination. The power to discriminate between the Truth and Untruth, between the appropriate and the inappropriate.

You have seen your colour, you have seen your figure, but you have not seen your true form. You can see your colour and figure with your eyes, but you can see your true form only in meditation.

You can mail your opinion or feedback on this book to: **books.feedback@tejgyan.org**

About Sirshree

Sirshree's spiritual quest, which began during his childhood, led him on a journey through various schools of philosophy and meditation practices. He studied a wide range of literature on mind science and spirituality. After a long period of deep contemplation on the truth of life, his quest culminated in attaining the ultimate truth.

Sirshree espouses, "All spiritual paths that lead to the truth begin differently but culminate at the same point – Understanding. This understanding is complete in itself. Listening to this understanding is enough to attain the Truth." Over the last two decades, he has dedicated his life to raise mass consciousness.

Sirshree has delivered more than 4000 discourses that throw light on this understanding. He has designed a system for wisdom, which makes it accessible to all. This system has inspired people from all walks of life to progress on their journey of the Truth. Thousands of seekers join in a virtual prayer for World Peace and Global Healing daily at 9:09 am and 9:09 pm.

About Tej Gyan Foundation

Tej Gyan Foundation is a non-profit organization founded on the teachings of Sirshree. The Foundation disseminates Tejgyan – the wisdom that guides one from self-development to Self-realization, leading towards Self-stabilization.

The Foundation's system for imparting wisdom has been assessed by international quality auditors and accredited with the ISO 9001:2015 certification. This wisdom has been presented in a simple, systematic, and practically applicable form that makes it accessible to people from all walks of life, regardless of religion, caste, social strata, country, or belief system.

The Foundation has centers in more than 400 cities and towns across India and other countries. The mission of Tej Gyan Foundation is to create a highly evolved society by leading seekers from negative thoughts to positive thoughts and further, from positive thoughts to Happy thoughts. A 'Happy thought' is the auspicious thought of being free from all thoughts, leading to the state of supreme bliss beyond thoughts.

If you seek such wisdom that leads you beyond mere knowledge, dissolves all problems, frees you from all limiting beliefs, reveals the true nature of divinity, and establishes you in the ultimate truth, then it is time to discover Tejgyan; it is time to rise above the mundane knowledge of words and experience Tejgyan!

The MahaAasmani Magic of Awakening Retreat

Self-development to Self-realization towards Self-stabilization

Do you wish to experience unconditional happiness that is not dependent on any reason? Happiness that is permanent and only increases with time? Do you wish to experience love, peace, self-belief, harmony in relationships, prosperity, and true contentment? Do you wish to progress in all facets of your life, viz. physical, mental, social, financial, and spiritual?

If you seek answers to these questions and are thirsty for the ultimate truth, then you are welcome to participate in the MahaAasmani Magic of Awakening retreat organized by Tej Gyan Foundation. This is the Foundation's flagship retreat based on the teachings of Sirshree.

The purpose of this retreat

The purpose of this retreat is that every human being should:

- Discover the answer to "Who am I" and "Why am I?" through direct experience and be established in ultimate bliss.

- Learn the art of living in the present, free from the burden of the past and the anxiety of the future.

- Acquire practical tools to help quieten the chattering mind and dissolve problems.

- Discover missing links in the practices of Meditation (*Dhyana*), Action (*Karma*), Wisdom (*Gyana*), and Devotion (*Bhakti*).

About Books by Sirshree

Sirshree's published work includes more than 150 book titles, some of which have been translated into more than 10 languages. His literature provides a profound reading on various topics of practical living and unravels the missing links in karma, wisdom, devotion, meditation, and consciousness.

His books have been published by leading publishing houses like Penguin, Hay House, Bloomsbury, Wisdom Tree, Jaico, etc. "The Source" book series, authored by Sirshree, has sold over 10 million copies. Various luminaries and celebrities like His Holiness the Dalai Lama, publishers Mr. Reid Tracy, Ms. Tami Simon and Yoga Master Dr. B. K. S. Iyengar have released Sirshree's books and lauded his work.

The Source
Attain Both, Inner Peace and Worldly success

Awaken the Power of Faith
Discover the 7 Principles of the Highest Power of the Universe

To order books authored by Sirshree, login to:
www.gethappythoughts.org
For further details, call: +91 9011013210

SELECT BOOKS AUTHORED BY SIRSHREE

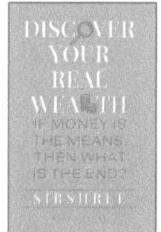
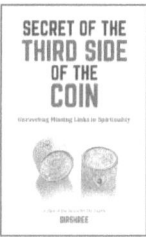

To order these and other books authored by Sirshree
Visit **www.gethappythoughts.org**

Tej Gyan Foundation – Contact details

Registered Office:
Happy Thoughts Building, Vikrant Complex, Near Tapovan Mandir, Pimpri, Pune 411017, INDIA. Contact: +91 20-27411240, +91 20-27412576

MaNaN Ashram:
Survey No. 43, Sanas Nagar, Nandoshi Gaon, Kirkatwadi Phata, Off Sinhagad Road, Taluka Haveli, Pune district - 411024, INDIA. Contact: +91 992100 8060.

WORLD PEACE PRAYER

Divine Light of Love, Bliss, and Peace is Showering;
The Golden Light of Higher Consciousness is Rising;
All negativity on Earth is Dissolving;
Everyone is in Peace and Blissfully Shining;
O God, Gratitude for Everything!

Members of Tej Gyan Foundation have been offering this impersonal mass prayer for many years. Those who are happy can offer this prayer. Those feeling low or suffering from illness can receive healing with this prayer.

If you are feeling troubled or sick, please sit to receive the healing effect of this prayer. Visualize that the divine white healing light is being showered on earth through the prayers of thousands and is also reaching you, bringing you peace and good health. You can dwell in this feeling for some time and then offer your gratitude to those offering the prayer.

A Humble Appeal

More than a million peace lovers pray for World Peace and Global Healing every morning and evening at 9:09. Also, a prayer (in Hindi) to elevate consciousness is webcast every day on YouTube at 3:30 pm and 9:00 pm IST. Please participate in this noble endeavor.

www.ingramcontent.com/pod-product-compliance
Lightning Source LLC
LaVergne TN
LVHW041705070526
838199LV00045B/1217